FAITH
BUILDERS
FOR
VICTORIOUS
LIVING

DECREE YOUR VICTORY

365 Day Devotional

LUCIA M. CLABORN

ISBN NUMBER
Paperback 979-8-9860477-0-6
EBook 979-8-9860477-2-0

Faith Builders for Victorious Living, 365 Day Devotional – Decree Your Victory
By Lucia M. Claborn
Published in the United States of America.
Lucia Claborn, LLC
2586 County Road 165, Moulton, Alabama 35650
www.LuciaClaborn.com

* It is the author's preference to capitalize personal pronouns referencing Deity in Bible verses.

Presented to:

_____

By:

_____

Occasion:

_____

DEDICATION

This book is lovingly dedicated to my Lord and Savior Jesus Christ because He gave me His Word to help me walk into victory when I was broken and living a defeated life. God promises to me are

"The Lord gave the Word: great was the company of those that published it." – Psalm 68:11, KJV

"...The women at home cry out the happy news!" – Tay

I am also dedicating this book to my husband, Danny, and our children, Daniel, McKenzie, Emily & Katie. They are my perfect gifts.

"Every good and perfect gift comes down from the Father of lights and is from above." James 1:17

TABLE OF CONTENTS

ACKNOWLEDGEMENTS

This book was created in 2004 as a daily calendar and over the years several people gave suggestions as to how it should be reformatted and published. All to no avail.

However, when God says it is time, He opens the door of opportunity. I want to thank Holy Spirit for encouraging me to not give up on my dream of seeing this devotional in print. I thank Him for directing and leading me to move on His promptings to re-edit and pursue the prize of being published to help others walk in victory and be a part of financing the Kingdom of God. The time has now come for publication.

I would like to thank Judith Taylor, my editor, and publisher. You are the vital part of making my dreams a reality. I do not want to be on this adventure with anyone else. Thank you for making my projects come to life.

And, Linda Starks, my friend, sister, and prayer warrior. Thank you for covering me, my business, and my projects in prayer. Thank you for proofreading my manuscripts.

Thank you both for helping make my dreams a reality.

INTRODUCTION

Faith comes by hearing and hearing the Word of God. God's Word portrays His thoughts and will for your life. He says you can *"Call to Me and I will answer you, and I will tell you great and mighty things, which you do not know." Jeremiah 33:3 – NASB.*

He says, *"So [it shall be] that he who invokes a blessing on himself in the land shall do so by saying. May the God of truth and fidelity [the Amen] bless me." Isaiah 65:16a – Amplified Bible.*

Romans 4:17, says *"to call those things which are not as though they are." – NASB.*

Job 22:28 says, *"Thou shalt also decree a thing, and it shall be established unto thee: and the light shall shine upon thy ways." – KJV*

With these verses in mind, as you read, meditate, and speak the daily faith decrees, your faith will grow to receive all the things God's Word tells you He has prepared for you.

When you make a decree from God's Word, you release great power from the Kingdom of Heaven to back up that decree. Psalm 81:10 confirms this, *"I am your only God, the living God. Wasn't I the one who broke the strongholds over you and raised you up out of bondage? Open your mouth with a mighty decree; I will fulfill it now, you'll see! The words that you speak, so shall it be!" – TPT*

As you decree God's Word, it will not return unto Him void. Isaiah 55:11 tells you, *"So will My word be which goes forth from My mouth; It will not return to Me empty, without accomplishing what I desire, and without succeeding in the matter for which I sent it." –* NASB

God desires for you, as His child, to walk in total victory by knowing who you are in Jesus, knowing what belongs to you, knowing His will for your life - which is His Word - so you can walk in victory and produce much fruit in your life.

As you travel through the pages of this devotional, my prayer is that you grow in God's wisdom, knowledge, understanding, and your faith will be elevated to a higher level. I pray that you realize God has given you the ability to live a victorious life because of the Covenant created with Jesus when He shed His Blood for you so you can enjoy freedom and walk in victory.

Be Blessed Abundantly More,
Lucia M. Claborn

BIBLE VERSIONS

AAT — The Bible: An American Translation (J.M. Powis Smith and Edgar J. Goodspeed)

ABPS — The Holy Bible Containing the Old and New Testaments: An Improved Edition (American Baptist Publication Society)

ABUV — The New Testament of Our Lord and Savior Jesus Christ, American Bible Union Version (John A. Broadus et al)

Alf — The New Testament (Henry Alford)

Amp — The Amplified New Testament

ASV — The American Standard Version

Bas — The New Testament in Basic English

Beck — The New Testament in the Language of Today (William F. Beck)

Ber — The Berkeley Version of the New Testament (Gerrit Berkuyl)

Con — The Epistles of Paul (W. J. Conybeare)

DeW — Praise-Songs of Israel: A Rendering of the Book of Psalms (John DeWitt)

Gspd — The New Testament: An American Translation (Edgar J. Goodspeed)

Har — The Psalms for Today: A New Translation from the Hebrew into Current English (R. K. Harrison)

Jerus — The Jerusalem Bible

JPS — The Holy Scriptures According to the Masoretic Text: A New Translation (The Jewish Publication Society)

KJV — King James Version

Knox — The New Testament in the Translation of Monsignor Ronald Knox

Lam — The New Testament According to the Eastern Texts (George M. Lamsa)

Message — The Message Bible

Mof — The New Testament: A New Translation (James Moffatt)

Mon — The Centenary Translation: The New Testament in Modern English (Helen Barrett Montgomery)

NAB — The New American Bible

NASB — The New American Standard Bible: New Testament

NEB — The New English Bible: New Testament

Nor — The New Testament: A New Translation (Olaf M. Norlie)

Phi — The New Testament in Modern English (J. B. Phillips)

Rhm — The Emphasized New Testament: A New Translation (J. B. Rotherham)

Rieu — The Book of Acts (C. H. Rieu) The Four Gospels (E. V. Rieu)

RSV — The Revised Standard Version

RV — The Holy Bible: Revised Version

Sept — The Septuagint (Charles Thomson)

Sprl — A Translation of the Old Testament Scriptures From the Original Hebrew (Helen Spurrell)

Tay — Living Letters: The Paraphrased Epistles; Living Gospels; The Paraphrased Gospels; Living Prophecies; The Minor Prophets Paraphrased and Daniel and the Revelation (Kenneth N. Taylor)

TCNT — The Twentieth Century New Testament

Tor — The Torah: The Five Books of Moses

Wey — The New Testament in Modern Speech (Richard Francis Weymouth)

Wms — The New Testament: A Translation in the Language of the People (Charles B. Williams)

YLT —Young's Literal Translation of the Holy Bible (Robert Young)

TOPICAL INDEX BY DATE

...yes, your promises rejuvenate me. Psalm 119:50a — Message

...Thy word giveth me life. — DeW

Healing
Jan 18
Jan 27
Feb 27
Mar 22
May 27
Jun 21
Jul 9
Jul 21
Jul 27
Aug 6
Aug 26
Sep 30
Oct 4
Oct 18
Nov 8
Nov 23

Holy Spirit
Jan 11
Mar 3
Mar 25
Apr 5
Apr 23
May 26
Jun 25
Aug 17
Aug 28
Sep 14
Nov 12

Joy
Feb 14
Feb 24
Apr 6
Apr 19
May 15

Joy Cont.
Jun 8
Aug 14
Nov 24

Love
Jan 10
Jan 20
Feb 3
Mar 11
Mar 19
Mar 30
Apr 13
Apr 17
Apr 18
May 9
Jun 10
Jun 20
Aug 10
Aug 22
Aug 30
Sep 28
Oct 6
Nov 1
Nov 15
Dec 1

Mercy
Feb 9
Feb 22
Sep 1
Oct 17

Patience
May 18
Jun 11
Jul 23
Aug 12

Peace
Jan 8
Feb 4
Feb 7
Mar 24
Mar 31
Apr 12
May 20
Jun 26
Aug 16
Sep 20
Oct 9
Nov 7
Dec 11
Dec 14
Dec 21

Power
Mar 4
Mar 10
May 23
Sep 10
Oct 24

Praise
Jan 6
Feb 19
Apr 2
Apr 25
May 11
May 24

Praise Cont.
Jun 2
Jul 1
Jul 15
Aug 4
Sep 2
Sep 4
Sep 19
Oct 1
Oct 19
Nov 5
Dec 16

Prosperity
Jan 3
Jan 21
Feb 11
Feb 26
Feb 28
Mar 8
Mar 12
Mar 29
Apr 8
Apr 15
Apr 20
Apr 21
Apr 30
May 7
May 12
May 14
Jun 3
Jun 5
Jun 13
Jun 22
Jun 29
Jul 3
Jul 7

JANUARY

But forget
all that—
it is nothing
compared to
what I am going
to do.
For I am
about to do
something new.
See, I have
already begun!
Do you not see it?
I will make a
pathway
through
the wilderness.
I will
create
rivers
in the dry
wasteland.
Isaiah 43:18-19

January 1 – The Lord Is My Salvation

Behold, God is my salvation: I will trust, and not be afraid: for the Lord Jehovah is my strength and my song; He also is become my salvation. Isaiah 12:2

Behold, God, my salvation! I will trust and not be afraid, for the Lord God is my strength and song; yes, He has become my salvation. — Amp

Yes, indeed - God is my salvation. I trust. I won't be afraid. God-yes God! - is my strength and song, best of all, my salvation! — Message

God is here to deliver me; I will go forward confidently, and not be afraid; source of my strength, theme of my praise; the Lord has made Himself my protector. — Knox

God indeed is my Savior, I am confident and unafraid. My strength and my courage is the Lord, and He has been my Savior. — NAB

...the Eternal is my strength...He has delivered me indeed. — Mof

I decree God is my Salvation. I decree He is my Strength, My Song, and my Deliverer. I will not be afraid because I am putting my trust and confidence in Jesus.

January 2 – Chosen By God

But ye are a chosen generation, a royal priesthood, a holy nation, a peculiar people; that ye should shew forth the praises of Him who hath called you out of darkness into His marvelous light. 1 Peter 2:9

But you are a chosen race, a royal priesthood, a dedicated nation, [God's] own purchased, special people that you may set forth the wonderful deeds and display the virtues and perfections of Him Who called you out of darkness into His marvelous light. — Amp

But you are the ones chosen by God, chosen for the high calling of priestly work, chosen to be a holy people, God's instruments to do His work and speak out for Him, to tell others of the night-and-day difference He made for you - from nothing to something, from rejected to accepted. — Message

...a consecrated nation, God's own people, entrusted with the proclamation of the goodness ... — TCNT

I decree I am God's special person, a chosen race, a royal priesthood. I decree I am delivered out of darkness into His marvelous light. I decree I am proclaiming His goodness to me. I decree I am displaying His great deeds of virtue and perfection in my life.

January 3 – Prosperous Future

Though thy beginning was small, yet thy latter end should greatly increase. Job 8:7

And though your beginning was small, yet your latter end would greatly increase. — Amp

Even though you're not much right now, you'll end up better than ever. — Message

Then, though thy beginning be small, thy end shall be exceeding great. — ABPS

Your former state will seem to you as nothing beside your new prosperity. — Jerus

A poor thing thy old prosperity will seem, matched with the abundance He gives thee now. — Knox

I decree that although my beginning may have been small, my future is full of abundant potential and prosperity. I decree today is my future. I decree I am believing I am receiving my abundance and prosperity now. I decree my end will be exceedingly great.

January 4 – Rejoice In The Lord

Rejoice in the Lord always: and again I say, Rejoice. Philippians 4:4

Rejoice in the Lord always [delight, gladden yourselves, in Him] again I say, Rejoice! — Amp

Celebrate God all day; every day. I mean revel in Him! — Message

Always be glad in the Lord... — Wey

All joy be yours at all times in your union with the Lord. — TCNT

By the help of the Lord always keep up the glad spirit. — Wms

Delight yourselves in the Lord... — Phi

Be happy in the Lord always... — Beck

I decree I am happy now because I am always delighting myself in the Lord. I decree I am celebrating Him today for who He is and what He is doing in my life. I decree I am full of joy because I spend time in His presence.

January 5 – I Am Righteousness

For He hath made Him to be sin for us who knew no sin; that we might be made the righteousness of God in Him. 2 Corinthians 5:21

For our sake He made Christ [virtually] to be sin who knew no sin, so that in and through Him we might become [endued with, viewed as being in, and examples of] the righteous of God [what we ought to be approved and acceptable and in right relationship with Him, by His goodness]. — Amp

God put the world square with Himself through the Messiah, giving the world a fresh start by offering forgiveness of sins. — Message

...that we might be changed into the righteousness of God in Christ. — Con

...so that in Him we might be turned into the holiness of God. — Knox

...so that in Him we might receive justification from God. — Nor

I decree I am having a fresh start today. I decree I am forgiven and holy just as Jesus is holy. I am righteous as Jesus is righteous. I decree I am seeing myself justified and in right standing with God. I decree God accepts me and approves of me today. He loves me.

January 6 – Praise The Lord

Enter into His gates with thanksgiving, and into His courts with praise: be thankful unto Him, and bless His name. Psalm 100:4

Enter into His gates with thanksgiving and a thank offering and into His courts with praise! Be thankful and say so to Him, bless and affectionately praise His name! — Amp

Enter with the password: "Thank You!" Make yourselves at home, talking praise. Thank Him. Worship Him. — Message

Enter His gates with rejoicing, and His precincts with praise... — Har

Give thanks unto Him, and bless His name... — ASV

I decree I am entering into His gates with thanksgiving and into His courts with praise. I decree I am thankful for Jesus. I decree I am blessing His Holy Name and I praise Him with all my heart for who He is in my life.

January 7 – See What God Is Doing

Where there is no vision, the people perish; but he that keepeth the law, happy is he. Proverbs 29:18

Where there is no vision [no redemptive revelation of God], the people perish; but he who keeps the law [of God, which includes that of man] - blessed (happy, fortunate, and enviable) is he. — Amp

If people cannot see what God is doing, they stumble all over themselves; but when they attend to what he reveals, they are most blessed. — Message

Where there is no prophecy the people cast off restraint, but blessed is he who keeps the law. — RSV

Without prophecy the people become demoralized; but happy is he who keeps the law. — NAB

Where there is no vision, the people run wild; but happy is he who keeps the law. — Ber

I decree I am walking in God's vision for my life, and I am happy. I decree I am receiving His Divine understanding and revelation of His plan for my life. I decree Holy Spirit is leading me into all truth. I decree I am blessed in everything I do.

January 8 – God's Peace

I will both lay me down in peace and sleep: for thou, Lord, only makest me dwell in safety.
Psalm 4:8

In peace I will both lie down and sleep, for You, Lord, alone make me dwell in safety and confident trust. — Amp

At day's end I am ready for sound sleep, for you, God, have put my life back together. — Message

Even as I lay down, sleep comes, and with sleep tranquility, what need, Lord, of aught but thyself to bring me confidence. — Knox

So quietly I lay me down to sleep for even alone, thanks to Thee, I am secure. — Mof

In peace I will lay me down. And at once will sleep for Thou, O Jehovah! When I am alone makest me to dwell securely. — DeW

As soon as I lay down, I fall peacefully asleep... — NAB

I decree I am confidently trusting in the Lord. I decree I am dwelling in safety and my mind is at peace. I decree when I lay down, I am sleeping peacefully. I decree I am secure in God.

January 9 – Record the Vision

And the Lord answered me, and said, write the vision, and make it plain upon tablets, that he may run that readeth it. For the vision is yet for the appointed time, but at the end it shall speak, and not lie: though it tarry, wait for it; because it will surely come, it will not tarry.
Habakkuk 2:2-3

And the Lord answered me and said, Write the vision and engrave it so plainly upon tablets that everyone who passes may [be able to] read [it easily and quickly] as he hastens by. For the vision is yet for an appointed time and it hastens to the end [fulfillment]; it will not deceive or disappoint. Though it tarry wait [earnestly] for it, because it will surely come; it will not be behind-hand on its appointed day. — Amp

And then God answered: "Write this. Write what you see. Write it out in big block letters so that it can be read on the run. This vision-message is a witness pointing to what's coming. It aches for the coming - it can hardly wait! And it does not lie. If it seems slow in coming, wait. It's on its way. It will come right on time. — Message

I decree God is giving me His vision for my life. I decree it speaks to me. I decree I am confident it is coming to pass right on time.

January 10 – Perfect Like Jesus

Herein is our love made perfect, that we may have boldness in the day of judgement: because as he is, so are we in this world. 1 John 4:17

In this [union and communion with Him] love is brought in completion and attains perfection with us, that we may have confidence for the Day of Judgment [with assurance and boldness to face Him], because as He is, so are we in this world. — Amp

This way, love has the run of the house, becomes at home and mature in us, so that we're free of worry on Judgment Day - our standing in the world is identical with Christ's. — Message

...when we have perfect confidence about... — Gspd

...since in this world we are living as He is... — Mof

...for we realize that our life in this world is actually His life lived in us... —Phi

I decree I am being made perfect in love. I decree God sees me as He sees Jesus. I decree I am in union with Jesus, so I am justified and sanctified. I decree I am confident and full of boldness as I stand before God.

January 11 – Living In The Spirit

If we live in the Spirit, let us also walk in the Spirit. Galatians 5:26

If we live by the [Holy] Spirit, let us also walk by the Spirit. [If by the Holy Spirit we have our life in God, let us go forward walking in line, our conduct controlled by the Spirit.]. — Amp

Since this is the kind of life we have chosen, the life of the Spirit, let us make sure that we do not just hold it as an idea in our heads or a sentiment in our hearts, but work out its implications in every detail of our lives. — Message

If we live by the Spirit, let our steps be guided by the Spirit... — Con

If we are living now by the Holy Spirit's power, let us follow the Holy Spirit's leading in every part of our lives. — Tay

I decree I am totally surrendering my life to Holy Spirit today. I decree He lives in me. I decree as I am walking with Him, He leads me, guides me, and directs me in every area and every detail of my life.

January 12 – The Mind Of Christ

For who hath known the mind of the Lord, that He may instruct him? But we have the mind of Christ. 1 Corinthians 2:16

For who has known or understood the mind (the counsels and purposes) of the Lord so as to guide and instruct him and give him knowledge? But we have the mind of Christ (the Messiah) and do hold the thoughts (feelings and purposes) of His heart. — Amp

Isaiah's question, "Is there anyone around who knows God's Spirit, anyone who knows what He is doing?" has been answered: Christ knows, and we have Christ's Spirit. — Message

For who has comprehended the mind of the Lord as to be able to instruct him? We, however, have the very mind of Christ. — TCNT

We who are spiritual have the very thoughts of Christ. — Phi

Well, our thoughts are Christ's thoughts. — Mof

I decree I have the mind of Christ. I decree I am thinking His thoughts. I decree I am now holding the thoughts, feelings, and purposes of His heart in my heart.

January 13 – God's Preservation

Thou art my hiding place; thou shalt preserve me from trouble; thou shalt compass me about with songs of deliverance. Selah. Psalm 32:7

You are a hiding place for me; You, Lord, preserve me from trouble, You surround me with songs and shouts of deliverance. Selah [pause, and calmly think of that]! — Amp

God's my island hideaway; keeps danger far from the shore, throws garlands of hosannas around my neck. — Message

Thou art a hiding place for me; from distress wilt thou preserve me, with shouts of deliverance wilt thou compass me about. — Rhm

Thou art a refuge for me from distress so that it cannot touch me, thou dost guard me and enfold me in salvation beyond all reach of harm. — NEB

Thou wilt preserve me from the adversary... — JPS

I decree the Lord is my Hiding Place. I decree He is surrounding me with songs and shouts of deliverance. I decree He is protecting me from harm and delivering me from Satan's schemes and plans.

January 14 – Give It Away Freely

And as ye go, preach, saying, the kingdom of heaven is at hand, heal the sick, cleanse the lepers, raise the dead, freely ye have received, freely give. Matthew 10:7-8

Cure the sick, raise the dead, cleanse the lepers, drive out demons. Freely (without pay) you have received, freely (without charge) give. — Amp

Bring health to the sick. Raise the dead. Touch the untouchables. Kick out the demons. You have been treated generously, so live generously. — Message

...keep on curing the sick... — Wms

...raise the dead, cleanse the lepers... — ASV

...bring the dead to life... — Rieu

...you have received free of cost, give free of cost. — TCNT

I decree I am healing the sick, raising the dead, and driving out demons in people's lives. I decree I have Holy Spirit and His power living inside of me. I decree I have received freely so I am giving freely.

January 15 – Trust God

Blessed is the man that trusteth in the Lord, and whose hope the Lord is. Jeremiah 17:7

[Most] blessed is the man who believes in, trusts in, and relies on the Lord, and whose hope and confidence the Lord is. — Amp

But blessed is the man who trusts me; God, the woman who sticks with God. — Message

Blessed shall he be that puts his trust in the Lord, makes the Lord his refuge. — Knox

Blessed is the man who trusts in the Lord, and rests his confidence upon Him. — NEB

A blessing on the man who puts his trust in Yahweh, with Yahweh for his hope. — Jerus

I decree I am trusting in the Lord. I decree I am blessed. I decree Jesus is my Lord. I decree He is my Confidence, my Hope, and my Refuge. I decree I am believing in and relying on Him with my whole heart.

January 16 – God's Protection

The angel of the Lord encampeth round about them that fear Him, and delivereth them. Psalm 34:7

The Angel of the Lord encamps around those who fear Him [who revere and worship Him with awe] and each of them He delivers. — Amp

God's angel sets up a circle of protection around us while we pray. —Message

The messenger of Yahweh encampeth around them who revere Him. Thus hath He delivered them. — Rhm

The Angel of Jehovah keepeth guard, around those that fear Him. And He delivereth them. — DeW

I decree I am encircled with a hedge of protection by God's angels as I worship Him and pray. I decree they protect me, guard me, and deliver me from the enemy's works as I reverence Him with a holy awe.

January 17 – God Cares For You

Casting all your care upon Him; for He careth for you. 1 Peter 5:7

Casting the whole of your care [all your anxieties, all your worries, all your concern, once and for all] on Him, for He cares for you affectionately and cares about you watchfully. — Amp

Live carefree before God; He is most careful with you. — Message

Let all your anxieties fall upon Him, His great interest is in you. — Mof

Throw back on Him the burden of all your anxiety, He is concerned for you. — Knox

...He takes care of you. — Beck

...you are His personal concern. — Phi

...He makes you His care. — TCNT

I decree I am casting all of my worries, fears, anxieties, concerns, and cares onto Jesus, once and for all, because He loves me. I decree He cares for me.

January 18 – Healed

Who His own self bare our sins in His own body on the tree that we, being dead to sins, should live unto righteousness: by whose stripes ye were healed. 1 Peter 2:24

He personally bore our sins in His [own] body on the tree [as on an altar and offered Himself on it], that we might die (cease to exist) to sin and live to righteousness. By His wounds you have been healed. — Amp

He used His servant body to carry our sins to the Cross so we could be rid of sin, free to live the right way. His wounds became your healing. — Message

...that we might break with sin and live the good life... — Mof

...by His wounds you have been healed. — NEB

...it was the suffering that He bore which has healed you. — Phi

I decree I am now dead to sin. I decree I am the righteousness of God through Christ Jesus. I decree I am receiving my healing because Jesus paid the price for me to be healed.

January 19 – Word Power

(As it is written, I have made thee a father of many nations,) before Him whom he believed, even God, who quickeneth the dead, and calleth those things which be not as though they were. Romans 4:17

As it is written, I have made you a father of many nations. [He was appointed our father] in the sight of God in Whom he believed. Who gives life to the dead and speaks of the non-existent things that [He foretold and promised] as if they [already] existed. — Amp

Abraham was first named "father" and then became a father because he dared to trust God to do what only God could do: raise the dead to life, with a word make something out of nothing. — Message

...and speaks of future events with as much certainty as though they were already past. — Tay

...and speak His word to those who are yet unborn. — Phi

I decree I am calling those things which are not as though they are, I decree I am trusting God to do what only He can do. I decree I am standing on God's promises. I decree I believe I am receiving them now.

January 20 – No Fear Here

For God has not given us the spirit of fear; but of power, and of love, and of a sound mind.
2 Timothy 1:7

For God did not give us a spirit of timidity (of cowardice, or craven and cringing and fawning fear), but [He has given us a spirit] of power and of love and of calm and well-balanced mind and discipline and self-control.
— Amp

God does not want us to be shy with His gifts, but bold and loving and sensible. — Message

The spirit He has bestowed on us is not one that shrinks from danger... — Knox

...but one of power and of love and of sound judgment.
— Wey

...but a spirit of power, love and self-control. — TCNT

...but one to inspire strength, love and self-discipline. — NEB

I decree I am living a self-disciplined life. God has given me a spirit full of love, power, and self-control. I decree I am calm. I decree I do not have a spirit of fear. I decree I am bold. I decree I do not shrink back from danger.

January 21 – Seed For The Sower

Now He that ministereth seed to the sower both minister bread for your food, and multiply your seed sown, and increase the fruits of your righteousness. 2 Corinthians 9:10

And [God] Who provides seed for the sower and bread for eating will also provide and multiply your [resources for] sowing and increase the fruits of your righteousness [which manifests itself in active goodness, kindness, and charity]. — Amp

The most generous God who gives seed to the farmer that becomes bread for your meals is more than extravagant with you. — Message

He who gives seed to the sower and turns that seed into bread to eat will give you the seed of generosity to sow and, for harvest, the satisfying bread of good deeds done. — Phi

...and enlarge the harvest which your deeds of charity yield. — Wms

I decree God is being extravagant with me. I decree He is generous to me and gives me seed to sow into His Kingdom. I decree the seeds I have sown are multiplying and producing a great harvest now.

January 22 – My Authority

Behold, I give unto you power to tread on ser-pents and scorpions, and over all the power of the enemy; and nothing shall by any means hurt you. Luke 10:19

Behold I have given you authority and power to trample upon serpents and scorpions, and [physical and mental strength and ability] over all the power that the enemy [possesses]; and nothing shall in any way harm you. — Amp

See what I have given you? Safe passage as you walk on snakes and scorpions, and protection from every assault of the Enemy. No one can put a hand on you. — Message

And now you see that I have given you power... — NEB

Now listen! I have given you authority... — Nor

It is true that I have given you power... — Phi

I decree I am walking in my God-given power and au-thority over every attack or assault of Satan and his demonic forces. I decree I am using my power and au-thority to enforce Satan's defeat. I decree no harm or backlash from Satan will come near me.

January 23 – I Can Do All Things

I can do all things through Christ which strengtheneth me. Philippians 4:13

I have strength for all things in Christ Who empowers me [I am ready for anything and equal to anything through Him Who infuses inner strength into me; I am self-sufficient in Christ's sufficiency]. — Amp

Whatever I have, wherever I am, I can make it through anything in the One who makes me who I am. — Message

I have strength for all things in Him which giveth me power. — Alf

Nothing is beyond my power in the strength of Him who makes me strong! — TCNT

I am ready for anything through the strength of the one who lives within me. — Phi

I decree I am walking in Christ's strength that is empowering me for anything that comes my way. I decree He is infusing me with His strength. I decree His power is living on the inside of me to accomplish all things.

January 24 – Fight The Good Fight

Fight the good fight of faith, lay hold on eternal life, whereunto thou art also called, and hast professed a good profession before many witnesses. 1 Timothy 6:12

Fight the good fight of faith; lay hold of the eternal life to which you were summoned and [for which] you confessed the good I decree [of faith] but before many witnesses. — Amp

Run hard and fast in the faith. Seize the eternal life, the life you were called to, the life you so fervently embraced in the presence of so many witnesses. — Message

Keep up the good fight of faith... — Wms

Run the great race of the Faith... — TCNT

Fight the worthwhile battle, keep your grip on that eternal life... — Phi

I decree the only fight I am fighting in my life is the good fight of faith. I decree I am seizing every day and living the faith life I was called to live. I decree I am standing firm in my faith.

January 25 – The Blood Of Jesus

In whom we have redemption through His Blood, the forgiveness of sins, according to the riches of His grace. Ephesians 1:7

In Him we have redemption (deliverance and salvation) through His Blood, the remission (forgiveness) of our offenses (shortcomings and trespasses), in accordance with the riches and the generosity of His gracious favor. — Amp

Because of the sacrifice of the Messiah, His Blood poured out on the altar of the Cross, we're a free people - free of penalties and punishments chalked up by all our misdeeds. And not just barely free, either. Abundantly free! —Message

It is through Him, at the cost of His own Blood, that we are redeemed, freely forgiven through that full and generous grace. — Phi

I decree I am free from past penalties and punishments! I am saved, forgiven, delivered, and redeemed by the Blood of Jesus. I decree all of my past, present, and future sins are forgiven. I decree I am walking in His generous grace every day.

January 26 – All Your Might

Whatsoever your hand findeth to do, do it with thy might... Ecclesiastes 9:10a

Whatever your hand finds to do, do it with all your might... — Amp

Whatever turns up, grab it and do it. And heartily! — Message

All that thy hand findeth to do, with thy power do... — YLT

Whatever thy hand finds to do, do with thy might... — ABPS

Whatever thy hand findeth to do, do it will all thy might... — Sept

Whatever comes to your hand to do, do with all your power... — Bas

Throw yourself in to any pursuit that may appeal to you... — Mof

I decree whatever appeals to me, I am pursuing it with my hands. I decree I am doing it with all my power and all my might. I decree I am not quitting, fainting, or giving up until I am finished.

January 27 – Indwelling Spirit

But the Spirit of Him that raised up Jesus from the dead dwell in you, He that raised up Christ from the dead shall also quicken your mortal bodies by His Spirit that dwelleth in you. Romans 8:11

And if the Spirit of Him Who raised up Jesus from the dead dwells in you, [then] He Who raised up Christ Jesus from the dead will also restore to life your mortal (short-lived, perishable) bodies through His Spirit Who dwells in you. — Amp

It stands to reason, doesn't it, that if the alive-and-present God who raised Jesus from the dead moves into your life, He'll do the same thing in you that He did in Jesus, bring you alive to Himself? — Message

...shall make alive [even] your death-doomed bodies... — Rhm

...will also make your dying bodily self-live by His indwelling Spirit in your lives. — Mon

I decree the same Spirit that raised Jesus from the dead is alive and living on the inside of me. I decree He is restoring my body to perfect health and making me alive.

January 28 – God's Energy
And Power

For it is God which worketh in you both to will and to do of His good pleasure. Philippians 2:13

[Not in your own strength] for it is God Who is all the while effectually at work in you [energizing and creating in you the power and desire] both to will and to work for His good pleasure and satisfaction and delight. — Amp

Be energetic in your life of salvation, reverent and sensitive before God. That energy is God's energy, and energy deep within you, God Himself willing and working at what will give Him the most pleasure. —Message

For it is God Himself whose power creates within you both the desire and the power to execute His gracious will. — Wey

I decree I am not walking in my own strength. I decree I have God's creative power working in me. I decree God's power is stirring up my desire to execute His perfect will for my life. I decree His energizing power is working in me. I decree He is enabling me to please Him in everything I do.

January 29 – Guard Your Heart

Keep thy heart with all diligence; for out of it are the issues of life. Proverbs 4:23

Keep and guard your heart with all vigilance and above all that you guard, for out of it flow the springs of life. — Amp

Keep vigilant watch over your heart; that's where life starts. — Message

With all watchfulness guard thine heart; for out of it flow the actions of life. — Sprl

Use all thy watchfulness to keep thy heart true; that is the fountain whence life springs. — Knox

Guard your heart more than any treasure, for it is the source of all life. — NEB

I decree I am guarding my heart with all diligence because out of it flows the source of all the issues and actions of my life.

January 30 – Great Reward

After these things the word of the Lord came unto Abram in a vision, saying, Fear not, Abram: I am Thy shield, and Thy exceeding great reward. Genesis 15:1

After these things, the word of the Lord came to Abram in a vision, saying, Fear not, Abram, I am your Shield, your abundant compensation, and your reward shall be exceedingly great. — Amp

After all these things, this word of God came to Abram in a vision: "Do not be afraid, Abram. I am your shield. Your reward will be grand!" — Message

...I will keep you safe and great shall be your reward. — Bas

...Fear not, Abram! I am your shield; I will make your reward very great. — NAB

...your reward is marvelously rich. — Ber

...I will defend you...give you great blessings. — Tay

I decree the Lord is my Shield, my Protection, and my Exceeding Great Reward. I decree He is my Defender. I decree He is daily rewarding me with great blessings.

January 31 – Boldness And Confidence

According to the eternal purpose which He purposed in Christ Jesus our Lord: in whom we have boldness and access with confidence by the faith of Him. Ephesians 3:11-12

In Whom, because of our faith in Him, we dare to have the boldness (courage and confidence) of free access (an unreserved approach to God with freedom and without fear). — Amp

All this is proceeding along lines planned all along by God and then executed in Christ Jesus. We trust in Him, we're free to say whatever needs to be said, bold to go wherever we need to go. — Message

...who gives us all our confidence, bids us come forward, emboldened by our faith in Him. — Knox

...now we can come fearlessly right into God's presence. — Tay

I decree I have boldness, freedom, confidence, and courage, through Christ Jesus, to go where I need to go. I decree I can come boldly and without fear right into God's presence. I decree I am putting my trust in Jesus.

FEBRUARY

*Such love
has no
fear,
because
perfect love
expels all
fear.
If we are
afraid,
it is for
fear of
punishment,
and this
shows that
we have not
fully
experienced
His
perfect
love.
I John 4:18*

February 1 – A New Creation

Therefore if any man be in Christ, he is a new creature: old things are passed away; behold, all things are become new. 2 Corinthians 5:17

Therefore if any person is [ingrafted] in Christ (the Messiah) he is a new creation (a new creature altogether); the old [previous moral and spiritual condition] has passed away. Behold, the fresh and new has come! — Amp

Now we look inside, and what we see is that anyone united with the Messiah gets a fresh start, is created new. The old life is gone; a new life burgeons! — Message

There is a new creation whenever a man comes to be in Christ, what is old has gone, the new has come. — Mof

I decree I am born again. I decree I am united with Jesus. I decree I am a new creation with a fresh start. I decree my old spirit man and his way of life are gone. I decree my spirit man is new, re-created in Christ Jesus.

February 2 – Stay Alert

Be sober, be vigilant; because your adversary the devil, as a roaring lion, walketh about, seeking whom he may devour. 1 Peter 5:8

Be well balanced (temperate, sober of mind), be vigilant and cautious at all time; for that enemy of yours, the devil, roams around like a lion roaring [in fierce hunger], seeking someone to seize upon and devour. — Amp

Keep a cool head. Stay alert. The Devil is poised to pounce, and would like nothing better than to catch you napping. Keep your guard up. — Message

Be calm and watchful... — Gspd

Exercise self-control, be watchful (because your adversary the devil) is prowling about eager to devour you. — TCNT

I decree I am well balanced in my mind. I decree I am vigilant and alert to Satan's plans to devour me. I decree I am keeping my guard up. I decree I am taking authority over his plans for my life in the Name of Jesus. I decree Satan is defeated in my life and I enforce his defeat right now.

February 3 – Tenderhearted

And be ye kind one to another, forgiving one another, even as God for Christ's sake hath forgiven you. Ephesians 4:32

And become useful and helpful and kind to one another, tenderhearted (compassionate, understanding, loving-hearted), forgiving one another [readily and freely], as God in Christ forgave you. — Amp

Be gentle with one another, sensitive. Forgiving one another as quickly and thoroughly as God in Christ forgave you. — Message

Be understanding, be as ready to forgive other as... — Phi

Ready to forgive one another, just as God, in Christ, forgave you. — TCNT

...forgiving one another, just as God has forgiven you because you belong to Christ. — Tay

I decree I am full of God's loving-kindness, His gentleness, compassion, understanding and unconditional love. I decree I am choosing to forgive others freely, and quickly, just as God quickly forgives me.

February 4 – Resting In Peace

The Lord shall fight for you, and ye shall hold your peace. Exodus 14:14

The Lord will fight for you, and you shall hold your peace and remain at rest. — Amp

God will fight the battle for you. And you? You keep your mouths shut! — Message

Yahweh will do the fighting for you... — Jerus

The Lord will make war for you... — Bas

...and ye shall remain quiet. — ABPS

...and you have only to keep still. — Mof

...and you won't need to lift a finger. — Tay

...be ye therefore silent. — Sept

I decree God is fighting all my battles for me. I decree I am being still, and I am full of peace. I decree I am keeping my mouth quiet and continually resting in God.

February 5 – Know Your Calling

Wherefore the rather, brethren, give diligence to make your calling and election sure: for if ye do these things, ye shall never fall. 2 Peter 1:10

Because of this brethren, be all the more solicitous and eager to make sure (to ratify, to strengthen, to make steadfast) your calling and election; for if you do this, you will never stumble or fall. — Amp

So friends, confirm God's invitation to you, His choice of you. Do not put it off; do it now. Do this, and you'll have your life on a firm footing. — Message

For this reason brethren, be all the more earnest to make certain of your calling and election for, so long as you practice these things, you will never stumble. — Wey

I decree I am choosing God's calling, plan, and purpose for my life. I decree I am determined to be steadfast. I decree I am strengthening my mind to be stable in what He is calling me to do. I decree I will not stumble or fall.

February 6 – Faith Walker

For we walk by faith, not by sight. **2 Corinthians 5:7**

For we walk by faith [we regulate our lives and conduct ourselves by our conviction or belief respecting man's relationship to God and divine things, with trust and holy fervor; thus we walk] not by sight or appearance. — Amp

It's what we trust in but do not yet see that keeps us going. — Message

For we guide our lives by faith, and not by what we see. — TCNT

For we guide ourselves by faith and not by external appearance. — Wey

For I have to lead my life in faith, without seeing Him. — Mof

I decree I am continuously living my life walking by faith. I decree I am not moved by what I see happening in the natural realm. I decree I am not moved by circumstances. I decree I am changing my circumstances with my faith-filled words.

February 7 – Pleasing Ways

When a man's ways please the Lord, He maketh even his enemies to be at peace with him. Proverbs 16:7

When a man's ways please the Lord, He makes even his enemies to be at peace with him. — Amp

When God approves of your life, even your enemies will end up shaking your hand. — Message

When the ways of man please the Eternal, He makes even his foes friends with him. — Mof

Live as the Lord would have thee live, and He will make even thy enemies into well-wishers. — Knox

When the Lord is pleased with a man's ways, He makes even his enemies to be at peace with him. — NAB

When Jehovah delights in one's ways, He causes even his enemies to be at peace with him. — ABPS

I decree I am living my life in ways that please God. I decree He is approving of my life. I decree my enemies are at peace with me and wish me well.

February 8 – I Am Carefree

Be careful for nothing; but in every thing by prayer and supplication with thanksgiving let your requests be made known unto God. Philippians 4:6

Do not fret or have any anxiety about anything, but in every circumstance and in everything, by prayer and petition (definite requests), with thanksgiving, continue to make your wants known to God. — Amp

Do not fret or worry. Instead of worrying, pray. Let petitions and praises shape your worries into prayers, letting God know your concerns. — Message

In nothing be anxious... — ASV

Let no care trouble you... — Con

Do not worry about anything... — Mon

Entertain no worry... — Ber

I decree I am free from anxiety, worry, or fretting. I decree I am free from fear in my life about anything. I decree I am praising God and thanking Him for His goodness to me as I bring all my wants and concerns to Him.

February 9 – God's Word In Me

The Lord will perfect that which concerneth me; Thy mercy, O Lord, endureth forever: forsake not the work of thine own hands. Psalm 138:8

The Lord will perfect that which concerns me; Your mercy and loving-kindness, O Lord, endure forever - forsake not the works of Your own hands. — Amp

Finish what you started in me, GOD. Your love is eternal – do not quit on me now. — Message

Yahweh will carry through my cause — O Yahweh! Thy lovingkindness is age-abiding. — Rhm

The Lord will fulfill His purposes for me; Thy steadfast love, O Lord, endures forever. — RSV

...leave not Thy work unfinished. — NEB

I decree God is perfecting everything that concerns me. I decree His mercy and loving-kindness endure forever. I decree He will finish the good work He started in me because He loves me.

February 10 – Invoke A Blessing

That he who blesseth himself in the earth shall bless himself in the God of truth... Isaiah 65:16

So [it shall be] that he who invokes a blessing on himself in the land shall do so by saying. May the God of truth and fidelity [the Amen] bless me... — Amp

Then whoever prays a blessing in the land will use my faithful name for the blessing... — Message

He who invokes a blessing on himself in the land shall do so by the God who name is Amen... — NEB

He who prays for blessing the land, now invokes the faithful God... — Mof

Whoever asks to be blessed on earth will ask to be blessed by the God of truth... — Jerus

I decree I am opening my mouth and speaking blessings over my life. I decree I am saying what God says. I decree I am blessing myself exceedingly abundantly above what I can ask or imagine today with all of God's best that He has for me.

February 11 – Abounding Grace

And God is able to make all grace abound toward you; that ye, always having all sufficiency in all things, may abound to every good work. 2 Corinthians 9:8

And God is able to make all grace (every favor and earthly blessing) come to you in abundance, so that you may always and under all circumstances and whatever the need be self-sufficient [possessing enough to require no aid or support and furnished in abundance for every good work and charitable donation]. — Amp

God can pour on the blessings in astonishing ways so that you're ready for anything and everything, more than just ready to do what needs to be done. — Message

God has power to shower all kinds of blessings upon you, so that, having, under all circumstances and on all occasions, all that you can need, you may be able to shower all kinds of benefits upon others. — TCNT

I decree I am having all my needs met by God's grace. I decree I am blessed with more than enough and with all kinds of blessings so I can be a blessing to give into others at all times.

February 12 – Speak Life

Death and life are in the power of the tongue: and they that love it shall eat the fruit thereof.
Proverbs 18:21

Death and life are in the power of the tongue, and they who indulge in it shall eat the fruit of it [for death or life]. — Amp

Words kill, words give life; they're either poison or fruit - you choose. — Message

Death and life are determined by the tongue: the talkative must take the consequences. — Mof

Of life and death, tongue holds the keys; use it lovingly, and it will require thee. — Knox

Those who love to talk will suffer the consequences. Men have died for saying the wrong thing. — Tay

Death and life are in the power of the tongue: those who make it a friend shall eat its fruit. — NAB

I decree I am only speaking life-giving words out of my mouth. I decree my tongue is full of life. I decree my words are producing good fruit in my life and the lives of others.

February 13 – Everlasting Life

Verily, verily, I say unto you. He that believeth on Me hath everlasting life. I am the bread of life. John 6:47-48

I assure you, most solemnly I tell you, he who believes in Me [who adheres to, trusts in, relies on, and has faith in Me] has (now possesses) eternal life. I am the Bread of Life [that gives life – the Living Bread]. — Amp

Whoever believes in Me has real life, eternal life. I am the Bread of Life. — Message

I tell you the truth, if you believe, you have everlasting life. — Beck

...I am the bread that gives life. — Gspd

...I am the Life-giving Bread. — TCNT

I decree I am believing Jesus. I decree I am adhering to Him. I decree I am trusting in and relying on Him. I decree I am believing He is my Bread of Life. I decree I am trusting Jesus. I decree I have faith in Him that He is giving me life.

February 14 – Fullness of Joy

Thou wilt shew me the path of life: in Thy presence is fullness of joy; at Thy right hand there are pleasures for evermore. Psalm 16:11

You will show me the path of life; in Your presence is fullness of joy, at Your right hand there are pleasures forevermore. — Amp

Now You've got my feet on the life path, all radiant from the shining of Your face. — Message

...in Thy right hand are pleasures for evermore. — RV

Thou wilt shew me the way of life, make me full of gladness in Thy presence; at Thy right hand are delights that will endure forever. — Knox

You will reveal the path of life to me, give me unbounded joy in Your presence, and at Your right hand everlasting pleasures. — Jerus

I decree I am spending time in God's presence, and I am full of His joy. I decree I am walking on the path God has created for me. I decree it leads me to an abundant life full of pleasures.

February 15 – Rejoice And Be Glad

This is the day which the Lord hath made; we will rejoice and be glad in it. Psalm 118:24

This is the day which the Lord has brought about; we will rejoice and be glad in it. — Amp

This is the very day God acted – let's celebrate and be festive! — Message

This is the day which the Lord has made; let us rejoice and be glad in it. — RSV

This is a day we owe to the Eternal; let us be glad and rejoice in it. — Mof

I decree I am rejoicing in this very good day that God has made for me! I decree I am celebrating His goodness and I decree I am exceedingly glad in it!

February 16 – Peacefulness

And He arose, and rebuked the wind, and said unto the sea, Peace, be still. And the wind ceased, and there was a great calm. Mark 4:39

And He arose and rebuked the wind and said to the sea, Hush now! Be still (muzzled)! And the wind ceased (sank to rest as if exhausted by its beating) and there was [immediately a great calm (a perfect peacefulness). — Amp

Awake now, He told the wind to pipe down and said to the sea, "Quiet! Settle down!" The wind ran out of breath; the sea became smooth as glass. — Message

And being aroused, He rebuked the wind... — NASB

...and said to the sea, Peace! Be still! — RSV

...the wind dropped, and there was a dead calm. — NEB

...the wind sank, and there was a perfect calm. — Wey

I decree I am rebuking the blowing winds of circumstances in my life. I decree I am telling them to be still, be at peace, and calm down. I decree they obey me, and I decree I am enjoying my victory!

February 17 – God's Goodness

Oh how great is Thy goodness, which Thou hast laid up for them that fear Thee; which Thou hast wrought for them that trust in Thee before the sons of men! Psalm 31:19

Oh, how great is Your goodness, which You have laid up for those who fear, revere, and worship You, goodness which You have wrought for those who trust and take refuge in You before the sons of men! — Amp

What a stack of blessing You have piled up for those who worship You, ready and waiting for all who run to You to escape an unkind world.— Message

How great is Thy goodness which Thou has hidden away for them who revere Thee... — Rhm

What wealth of kindness Thou hast laid up for Thy worshipers... — Mof

I decree I am blessed beyond measure today with all of God's goodness. I decree I am worshipping Him. I decree I stand before Him in holy reverence, fear, and honor for who He is in my Life. I decree I am trusting Him and taking refuge in Him. I decree His works are marvelous.

February 18 – Abundant Grace

For if by one man's offence death reigned by one; much more they which receive abundance of grace and of the gift of righteousness shall reign in life by one, Jesus Christ. Romans 5:17

For if because of one man's trespass (lapse, offense) death reigned through that one, much more surely will those who receive [God's] overflowing grace (unmerited favor) and the free gift of righteousness [putting them into right standing with Himself] reign as kings in life through the one Man Jesus Christ (the Messiah, the Anointed One). — Amp

Here it is in a nutshell: Just as one person did it wrong and got us in all this trouble with sin and death, another person did it right and got us out of it. But more than just getting us out of trouble, He got us into life! — Message

All the more will those who receive God's overflowing mercy and gift of uprightness live and reign through the one individual Jesus Christ. — Gspd

I decree I am receiving God's life and grace today. I decree I am walking in His unmerited favor. I decree I am enjoying His free gift of righteousness. I decree I am in right standing with Father God.

February 19 – Sing Praises

I will praise the Lord according to His right-eousness: and will sing praise to the name of the Lord most high. Psalm 7:17

I will give to the Lord the thanks due to His rightness and justice, and I will sing praise to the name of the Lord Most High. — Amp

I am thanking God, who makes things right. I am singing the fame of heaven-high God. — Message

I will ever thank the Lord for His just retribution, singing praises to the name of the Lord, the most High. — Knox

I shall praise the Lord for His loving kindness, I shall sing to the name of the Lord Most High. — Sept

I will give to the Lord the thanks due to His righteousness, and I will sing praise to the name of the Lord, the Most High. — RSV

I will commend the Lord for His justice; I will sing praise to the name of the Lord Most High. — Har

I decree I am loving You, Lord! I decree I am thanking You for Your goodness and loving-kindness to me. I am praising You, Lord!

February 20 – Joy In Believing

And having confidence, I know that I shall abide and continue with you all for your furtherance and joy of faith. Philippians 1:25

Since I am convinced of this, I know that I shall remain and stay by you all, to promote your progress and joy in believing. — Amp

So I plan to be around awhile, companion to you as your growth and joy in this life of trusting God continues. — Message

Yes, I am confident that this is so ... to promote your progress and joy in the Faith. — TCNT

...to help you to develop and to be glad in your faith. — Gspd

...to the happy furtherance of your faith. — Knox

I decree I am walking in more confidence today. I decree I am living my life with more joy because I am believing God! I decree I am trusting Him, so my joy is full to overflowing!

February 21 – Renewed Day By Day

For which cause we faint not; but though our outward man perish, yet the inward man is renewed day by day. 2 Corinthians 4:16

Therefore we do not become discouraged (utterly spiritless, exhausted, and wearied out through fear). Though our outer man is [progressively] decaying and wasting away, yet our inner self is being [progressively] renewed day after day. — Amp

Even though on the outside it often looks like things are falling apart on us, on the inside, where God is making new life, not a day goes by without His unfolding grace. — Message

Therefore, as I said, we do not lose heart. No, even though outwardly as we are wasting away, yet inwardly we are being renewed day by day. — TCNT

No, we do not play the coward though the outward part of our nature is being worn down, our inner life is refreshed from day to day. — Knox

I decree I am not losing heart. I decree I am progressively renewing and refreshing my inner man with God's Word day by day.

February 22 – Wisdom Words

My mouth shall speak of wisdom and the meditation of my heart shall be of understanding.
Psalm 49:3

My mouth shall speak wisdom; and the meditation of my heart shall be understanding. — Amp

I set plainspoken wisdom before you, my heart-seasoned understandings of life. — Message

My mouth speaketh wisdom; the utterance of my heart is discernment.— DeW

My mouth shall speak wisdom; prudence shall be the utterance of my heart. — NAB

My lips have wisdom to utter; my heart whispers sound sense. — Jerus

For the words that I speak are wise, my thoughtful heart is full of understanding. — NEB

I decree I am speaking words that are full of wisdom. I decree the meditations of my heart are causing me to overflow with supernatural understanding and discernment.

February 23 – Faith By Works

Even so faith, if it hath not works, is dead, being alone. James 2:17

So also faith, if it does not have works (deeds and actions of obedience to back it up), by itself is destitute of power (inoperative, dead). — Amp

Does merely talking about faith indicate that a person really has it? — Message

So also faith, if it is unaccompanied by obedience... — Wey

In just the same way faith, if not followed by actions is, by itself, a lifeless thing. — TCNT

...if it does not lead to action... — NEB

...is dead in itself. — ASV

I decree I am revealing my faith is active and alive beyond my words. I decree I am obedient to put actions to my words by the works that I am putting my hands to accomplish.

February 24 – Full Joy

These things have I spoken unto you, that My joy might remain in you, and that your joy might be full. John 15:11

I have told you these things, that My joy and delight may be in you, and that your joy and gladness may be of full measure and complete and overflowing. — Amp

I've told you these things for a purpose: that My joy might be your joy, and your joy wholly mature. — Message

All this have I told you... — Knox

...so that My own joy may be yours... — TCNT

...that the joy which I have had... — Wms

...so that you can share My joy... — Phi

...may be made full. — ASV

...and that your joy may become perfect. — Wey

I decree I am stirring up the gift of joy inside of me. I decree I am full to overflowing with the joy of the Holy Spirit. I decree I have a full measure of Jesus' joy today. I decree my joy is totally complete.

February 25 – Wisdom Brings Happiness

Happy is the man that findeth wisdom, and the man that geteth understanding. Proverbs 3:13

Happy (blessed, fortunate, enviable) is the man who finds skillful and godly Wisdom, and the man who gets understanding [drawing it forth from God's Word and life's experiences]. — Amp

You're blessed when you meet Lady Wisdom, when you make friends with Madame Insight. — Message

Happy the man whose treasure-trove is wisdom, who is rich in discernment. — Knox

Happy is the man who gathers wisdom, the man who gains knowledge. — Mof

Blessed is the man who has found wisdom, the man who obtains understanding. — Ber

I decree I am gaining skillful, Godly wisdom and insight. I decree I am happy - blessed, fortunate, enviable - because I am drawing from God's wisdom and His understanding.

February 26 – Spiritual Blessings

Blessed be the God and Father of our Lord Jesus Christ, who hath blessed us with all spiritual blessings in heavenly places in Christ. Ephesians 1:3

May blessing (praise, laudation, and eulogy) be to the God and Father of our Lord Jesus Christ (the Messiah) Who has blessed us in Christ with every spiritual (given by the Holy Spirit) blessing in the heavenly realm! — Amp

How blessed is God! And what a blessing He is! He's the Father of our Master, Jesus Christ, and takes us to the high places of blessing in Him. — Message

...who has blessed us on high with every spiritual blessing, in Christ. — TCNT

...who has crowned us with every spiritual blessing in the heavenly realms in Christ. — Wey

I decree I am blessing Father God because He is blessing me with His anointing. I decree He is blessing me with every spiritual blessing in the Heavenly realm in Christ Jesus. I decree I am believing that I receive them now.

February 27 – Lay Hands On The Sick

...they shall lay hands on the sick, and they shall recover. Mark 16:18b

...they will lay their hands on the sick, and they will get well. — Amp

...they will lay hands on the sick and make them well. — Message

...they will lay hands on the sick and make them well. — Mof

I decree I am anointed. I decree that my hands are anointed. I decree I am laying hands on the sick and they are recovering in the authority of the Name of Jesus.

February 28 – Established Thoughts

Commit thy works unto the Lord, and thy thoughts shall be established. Proverbs 16:3

Roll your works upon the Lord [commit and trust them wholly to Him; He will cause your thoughts to become agreeable to His will, and] so shall your plans be established and succeed. — Amp

Put God in charge of your work, then what you've planned will take place. — Message

Commit thy works unto Jehovah, and thy purposes shall be established. — ASV

Roll your work onto the Lord and your plans will be achieved. — BER

Commit to the Lord all that you do, and your plans will be fulfilled. — NEB

Commit your business to the Lord; and your plans will prosper. — AAT

I decree I am committing the works my hands to the Lord. I decree I am trusting Him with everything I set my mind to do. I decree my thoughts are His thoughts, so I am prospering and accomplishing all of my plans.

February 29 – God's Strength

The Lord God is my strength and He will make my feet like hinds' feet and He will make me to walk upon mine high places. Habakkuk 3:19

The Lord God is my Strength, my personal bravery, and my invincible army; He makes my feet like hinds' feet and will make me to walk [not to stand still in terror, but to walk] and make [spiritual] progress upon my high places [of trouble, suffering or responsibility]! — Amp

Counting on God's Rule to prevail, I take heart and gain strength. I run like a deer. I feel like I am king of the mountain! — Message

The Lord God is my Strength, and He will give me the speed of a deer and bring me safely over the mountains. — Tay

The Lord God is my strength, and will guide my feet to the end. He maketh me walk in high places; that I may triumph with his song. — Sept

I decree I am walking in God's strength. I decree His strength is my strength. I decree He is causing me to walk above and triumph over all of life's challenges, troubles, and sufferings with the speed of a deer. I decree He is giving me His victory song!

MARCH

*For
everything
there
is
a
season,
a
time
for
every
activity
under
heaven.
Ecclesiastes 3:1*

March 1 – Faith Without Works

Yea, a man may say, Thou hast faith, and I have works: shew me thy faith without thy works, and I will shew thee my faith by my works. James 2:18

But someone will say [to you then], You [say you] have faith, and I have [good] works. Now you show me your [alleged] faith apart from any [good] works [if you can], and I by [good] works [of obedience] will show you my faith. — Amp

You can no more show me your works apart from your faith than I can show you my faith apart from my works. — Message

Someone indeed may say, You are a man of faith, and I am a man of action; then show me your faith, I reply, apart from any actions, and I will show you my faith by my actions. — TCNT

...show me thy faith apart from thy works and I by my works will show thee my faith. — ASV

I decree I am showing people my faith through my actions and works of obedience. I decree they are a reflection of my faith. I decree everything I put my hands to do, I release my faith to achieve it.

March 2 – No Respecter Of Persons

Then Peter opened his mouth, and said, Of a truth I perceive that God is no respecter of persons. Acts 10:34

And Peter opened his mouth and said: Most certainly and thoroughly I now perceive and understand that God shows no partiality and is no respecter of persons. — Amp

God plays no favorites! It makes no difference who you are or where you're from. — Message

I decree I am understanding that God is no respecter of persons. He is not show partiality. I decree what He is doing for someone else, He will do the same thing for me.

March 3 – The Gift Of Holy Spirit

Then Peter said unto them, Repent, and be baptized every one of you in the name of Jesus Christ for the remission of sins, and ye shall receive the gift of the Holy Ghost. Acts 2:38

And Peter answered them. Repent (change your views and purpose to accept the will of God in your inner selves instead of rejecting it) and be baptized, every one of you, in the name of Jesus Christ for the forgiveness of and release from your sins; and you shall receive the gift of the Holy Spirit. — Amp

Peter said, "Change your life. Turn to God and be baptized, each of you in the name of Jesus Christ, so your sins are forgiven. Receive the gift of the Holy Spirit." — Message

...then you also shall receive the gift, the Holy Spirit. — Tay

I decree I am repenting of all of my sins, and I am forgiven. I decree I have been baptized in the name of Jesus Christ, and I am thanking Father God, for the free gift of Holy Spirit. I decree I receive Him now!

March 4 – Holy Ghost Power

But ye shall receive power, after that the Holy Ghost is come upon you... Acts 1:8a

But you shall receive power (ability, efficiency, and might) when the Holy Spirit has come upon you... — Amp

...you will be baptized in the Holy Spirit... — Message

But you shall receive power when the Holy Spirit has come upon you... — NAB

I decree I am baptized in the Holy Spirit. I am receiving His power and His ability that is living on the inside of me and comes upon me for others.

March 5 – God's Greatness

Thine, O Lord, is the greatness, and the power, and the glory, and the victory, and the majesty... 1 Chronicles 29:11a

Yours, O Lord, is the greatness and the power and the glory and the victory and the majesty... — Amp

To you, O God, belong the greatness and the might, the glory, the victory, the majesty, the splendor... — Message

Thine, Lord, the magnificence, thine the power, splendour and glory and majesty are thine... — Knox

...the greatness, the power, the glory, the preeminence, and the majesty... — Ber

...Greatness and Might and Beauty and Victory and Majesty... — Rhm

I decree I am giving the Lord Jesus Christ all the honor for who He is in my life. I decree I give Him all of my praise. I decree He has all the greatness, power, glory, majesty, and victory. I decree I bless you today, Jesus.

March 6 – True Worship

But the hour cometh, and now is, when the true worshippers shall worship the Father in spirit and in truth: for the Father seeketh such to worship Him. John 4:23

A time will come, however, indeed it is already here, when the true (genuine) worshipers will worship the Father in spirit and in truth (reality); for the Father is seeking just such people as these as His worshipers. — Amp

Those who worship Him must do it out of their very being, their spirits, their true selves, in adoration. — Message

...will worship the Father in Spirit and in reality... — Mof

...in the true way of the spirit... — Bas

...the Father is looking for such people to worship Him. — Beck

I decree I am a true worshiper. I decree I worship You with great adoration, Father God. I decree I am worshiping You with my spirit man in complete truth. I decree I adore You with my whole heart.

March 7 – A Living Sacrifice

I beseech you therefore, brethren, by the mercies of God, that ye present your bodies a living sacrifice, holy, acceptable unto God, which is your reasonable service. Romans 12:1

I appeal to you therefore, brethren, and beg of you in view of [all] the mercies of God to make a decisive dedication of your bodies - presenting all your members and faculties - as a living sacrifice, holy (devoted, consecrated) and well pleasing to God which is your reasonable (rational, intelligent) service and spiritual worship. — Amp

So here's what I want you to do, God helping you: take your everyday, ordinary life - your sleeping, eating, going-to-work, and walking around life - and place it before God as an offering. — Message

I decree I am making myself a living sacrifice to You, God. I decree everything I do, Lord, I do it for Your glory. I decree I am devoting myself to You and consecrating myself for Your service and spiritual worship.

March 8 – An Expected End

For I know the thoughts that I think toward you, saith the Lord, thoughts of peace, and not of evil, to give you an expected end. Jeremiah 29:11

For I know the thoughts and the plans that I have for you, says the Lord, thoughts and plans for welfare and peace and not for evil, to give you hope in your final outcome. — Amp

I know what I am doing. I have it all planned out - plans to take care of you, not abandon you, plans to give you the future you hope for. — Message

I have not lost sight of My plans for you, the Lord says, and it is your welfare I have in mind, not your undoing; for you, too, I have a destiny and a hope. — Knox

I decree all of God's plans for me are good. I decree He will not harm me. I decree He is taking good care of me. I decree He wants me to prosper and be in peace. I decree He has a great future in store for me.

March 9 – Finish A Good Work

Being confident of this very thing, that He which hath begun a good work in you will perform it until the day of Jesus Christ. Philippians 1:6

Will continue until the day of Jesus Christ - right up to the time of His return - developing [that good work] and perfecting and bringing it to full completion in you. — Amp

There has never been the slightest doubt in my mind that the God who started this great work in you would keep at it and bring it to a flourishing finish on the very day Christ Jesus appears. — Message

Will keep right on helping you, grown in His grace until His task within you is finally finished on that day when Jesus Christ returns. — Tay

I decree I am confident that the great work God has begun in me, He is faithful to perfect it. I decree He will keep working on it, then bring it to a flourishing completeness when Jesus returns.

March 10 – God Is My Refuge

But I will sing of Thy power; yea, I will sing aloud of Thy mercy in the morning: for thou hast been my defence and refuge in the day of my trouble. Psalm 59:16

But I will sing of Your mighty strength and power; yes I will sing aloud of Your mercy and loving-kindness in the morning; for You have been to me a defense (a fortress and a high tower) and a refuge in the day of my distress. — Amp

And me? I am singing your prowess, shouting at cockcrow your largesse. For you've been a safe place for me, a good place to hide. — Message

But as for me I will sing of Thy might; and will sing aloud of Thy loving-kindness in the morning. — ABPS

...thou hast been my strong tower; a sure retreat in days of trouble. — NEB

I decree I am singing praises to Your Name this morning, Lord. You alone are my Refuge, my Fortress, and my High Tower. I decree Your mercy and loving-kindness keep me safe in times of trouble.

March 11 – Growing Up In All Things

But speaking the truth in love, may grow up into Him in all things, which is the head, even Christ. Ephesians 4:15

Rather, let our lives lovingly express truth in all things - speaking truly, dealing truly, living truly. — Amp

God wants us to grow up, to know the whole truth and tell it in love-like Christ in everything. — Message

But that we should live in truth and love and should grow up in every part to the measure of His growth, who is our head, even Christ. — Con

I decree I am growing up spiritually in Christ Jesus. I decree He is enabling me to speak the truth in love in everything I do and say so that I am more like Him.

March 12 – A Sun And Shield

For the Lord God is a sun and shield: the Lord will give grace and glory: no good thing will He withhold from them that walk uprightly.
Psalm 84:11

For the Lord God is a Sun and Shield; the Lord bestows [present] grace and favor and [future] glory (honor, splendor, and heavenly bliss)! No good thing will He withhold from those who walk uprightly. — Amp

All sunshine and sovereign is God, generous in gifts and glory. He does not scrimp with His traveling companions. — Message

Sun to enlighten, shield to protect us, the Lord God has favour, has honour to bestow. To innocent lives He will never refuse His bounty. — Knox

I decree I am the righteousness of God in Christ Jesus, and He has generous gifts of abounding blessings, favor, and honor in store for me. I decree He does not scrimp with me, and I believe I receive those generous gifts and blessings now.

March 13 – Not My Battle

Thus saith the Lord unto you, Be not afraid nor dismayed by reason of this great multitude; for the battle is not yours, but God's. 2 Chronicles 20:15

Be not afraid or dismayed at this great multitude; for the battle is not yours, but God's. — Amp

You won't have to lift a hand in this battle; just stand firm, Judah and Jerusalem, and watch God's saving work for you take shape. — Message

...fear not, falter not before this vast army: it is for God, not for you to fight them. — Mof

...have no fear; do not be dismayed by this great horde, for the battle is in God's hands, not yours. — NEB

I decree I am not in fear of any circumstance or situation in my life. I decree I am standing firm and standing still as I watch God fight all my battles for me.

March 14 – God's Love

And to know the love of Christ, which passeth knowledge, that ye might be filled with all the fullness of God. Ephesians 3:19

[That you may really come] to know [practically, through experience for yourselves] the love of Christ, which far surpasses mere knowledge [without experience]; that you may be filled [through all your being] unto all the fullness of God [may have the richest measure of the divine Presence, and become a body wholly filled and flooded with God Himself]! — Amp

And I ask Him that with both feet planted firmly on love, you'll be able to take in with all Christians the extravagant dimensions of Christ's love. — Message

And to know for yourselves that love so far beyond our comprehension, through all your being with God Himself. — Phi

I decree I am experiencing God's love for me. I decree it surpasses all my understanding. I decree I am being filled to overflowing, with His presence and His goodness. I decree I am standing in His love as it floods my spirit man. I decree I know He loves me.

March 15 – The Finisher Of Our Faith

Looking unto Jesus the author and finisher of our faith... Hebrews 12:2a

Looking away [from all that will distract] to Jesus, Who is the Leader and the Source of our faith [giving the first incentive for our belief] and is also its Finisher [bringing it to maturity and perfection] ... — Amp

Keeping your eyes on Jesus, who both began and finished this race we're in... — Message

Simply fixing our gaze upon Jesus, the Leader and Perfecter of faith... — Wey

Looking onward unto Jesus, the forerunner and the finisher of our faith... — Con

...our leader and example of faith... — Gspd

I decree I am keeping my eyes on Jesus and looking away from every distraction. I decree He is the author and finisher of my faith. I decree I am finishing the race that is set before me so I will be mature and perfect, lacking nothing. I decree Jesus is the example for my faith.

March 16 – Forgotten Sins

I, even, I am He that blotteth out thy trans-gressions for Mine own sake, and will not re-member thy sins. Isaiah 43:25

I, even I, am He Who blots out and cancels your transgressions, for My own sake, and I will not remember your sins. — Amp

But I, yes I, am the one who takes care of your sins - that's what I do. I do not keep a list of your sins. — Message

Yet it is I who (for My own sake) blot out your ill deeds, I put your sins out of My mind. — Mof

I alone, I am He, who for His own sake wipes out your transgressions, who will remember your sins no more. — NEB

I decree God has forgiven all of my sins. I decree they are blotted out, cancelled from my life. I decree God does not remember them anymore. I decree I choose to forgive myself, release all my self-condemning thoughts and I receive God's grace and mercy.

March 17 – Get Wisdom

How much better is it to get wisdom than gold! And to get understanding rather to be chosen than silver! Proverbs 16:16

How much better it is to get skillful and godly Wisdom than gold! And to get understanding is to be chosen rather than silver. — Amp

Get wisdom - it's worth more than money; choose insight over income every time. — Message

To acquire wisdom how much better than gold! And to get hold of understanding more choice than silver! — Rhm

To get wisdom is better than gold; to get understanding is to be chosen rather than silver. — RSV

Better gain wisdom than gold, choose discernment rather than silver. — Jerus

I decree God is giving me His wisdom in the affairs of my life because I am asking for a generous supply. I decree I am using His discernment and understanding to make wise decision in my life.

March 18 – Be Transformed

And be not conformed to this world; but be ye transformed by the renewing of your mind, that ye may prove what is the good, and acceptable, and perfect will of God. Romans 12:2

Do not be conformed to this world - this age, fashioned after and adapted to its external, superficial customs; but be ye transformed (changed) by the [entire] renewal of your mind - by its new ideals and its new attitude, so that you may prove [for yourselves] what is the good and acceptable and perfect will of God, even the thing which is good and acceptable and perfect [in His sight for you]. — Amp

Do not become so well-adjusted to your culture that you fit into it without even thinking. Instead, fix your attention on God. You'll be changed from the inside out. Readily recognize what he wants from you, and quickly respond to it. — Message

I decree I am not conforming my mind to the world around me. I decree I am renewing my mind every day with God's Word so I know His perfect will for my life. I decree I am transforming my mind daily, so I know what His plan is for my life.

March 19 – Fruit Of The Spirit

But the fruit of the Spirit is love, joy, peace, longsuffering, gentleness, goodness, faith, meekness, temperance: against such there is no law. Galatians 5:22-23

But the fruit of the [Holy] Spirit [the work which His presence within accomplishes] is love, joy (gladness), peace, patience (an even temper, forbearance), kindness, goodness (benevolence), faithfulness. Gentleness (meekness, humility), self-control (self-restraint, continence). Against such things there is no law [that can bring a charge]. — Amp

But what happens when we live God's way? He brings gifts into our lives, much the same way that fruit appears in an orchard - things like affection for others, exuberance about life, serenity. We develop a willingness to stick with things, a sense of compassion in the heart, and a conviction that a basic holiness permeates things and people. We find ourselves involved in loyal commitments, not needing to force our way in life, able to marshal and direct our energies wisely. — Message

I decree I am yielding to Holy Spirit, allowing His presence to fill me full of love, joy, peace, patience, kindness, self-control, generosity, tolerance, faithfulness, gentleness, and meekness. I decree I am not forcing my way in life.

March 20 – The New Man

And that ye put on the new man, which after God is created in righteousness and true holiness. Ephesians 4:24

And put on the new nature (the regenerate self) created in God's image. [Godlike] in true righteousness and holiness. — Amp

And then take on an entirely new way of life – a God fashioned life, a life renewed from the inside and working itself into your conduct as God accurately reproduces His character in you. — Message

And that you must clothe yourselves in that new nature which was created to resemble God, with the righteousness and holiness springing from the Truth. — TCNT

To put on the clean fresh clothes of the new life which was made by God's design for righteousness and the holiness which is no illusion. — Phi

I decree I am renewing my mind with God's Word. I decree I am taking on a new way of life. I decree I am changing from the inside out. I decree my character is revealing God's character within me. His righteousness and holiness are living inside of me.

March 21 – Yes And Amen

For all the promises of God in Him are yea, and in Him Amen, unto glory of God by us. 2 Corinthians 1:20

For as many as are the promises of God, they all find their Yes [answer] in Him [Christ]. For this reason we also utter the Amen (so be it) to God through Him [in His Person and by His agency] to the glory of God. — Amp

Whatever God has promised gets stamped with the Yes of Jesus. In Him, this is what we preach and pray, the great Amen. — Message

For, many as were the promises of God, in Christ is the Yes that fulfills them, therefore, through Christ again, let the Amen rise, through us, to the glory of God. — TCNT

For in Him is the yes that affirms all the promises of God, Hence it is through Him that we affirm our amen in worship. — Mof

I decree I am believing that I am receiving all of God's answers and promises that are found in Jesus Christ, the Anointed One. I decree I am receiving them now. I decree they are fulfilled in my life and will show forth His great Glory.

March 22 – Complete Healing

Who forgiveth all thine iniquities; who healeth all thy diseases. Psalm 103:3

Who forgives [every one of] all your iniquities. Who heals [each one of] all your diseases. — Amp

He forgives your sins - everyone. He heals your diseases - everyone. — Message

How He pardons all thy sins, heals all thy moral ills. — Knox

Who forgives all my guilt, who heals all my sicknesses. — AAT

In forgiving all your offences, in curing all your diseases. — Jerus

I decree I am walking in divine health. I decree Jesus is forgiving me of all of my sins, and He is healing all, yes, every one of the sicknesses and diseases attacking me mentally and in my physical body.

March 23 – We Are Over-Comers

And Caleb stilled the people before Moses, and said, Let us go up at once, and possess it; for we are well able to overcome it. Numbers 13:30

Caleb quieted the people before Moses, and said, let us go up at once and possess it; we are well able to conquer it. — Amp

Caleb interrupted, called for silence before Moses and said, "Let's go up and take the land - now. We can do it." — Message

And now, to still the rising outcry against Moses, Caleb spurred the people on to invade the land and conquer it, it is ready to fall into your hands. — Knox

I decree and I believe I have the same spirit in me that resided in Caleb. I decree I am more than a conqueror! I decree I cannot fail. I decree I am possessing my promises from God right now. I decree I am taking my land. I decree I can do it now!

March 24 – Perfect Peace

Thou wilt keep him in perfect peace, whose mind is stayed on Thee: because he trusteth in Thee. Isaiah 26:3

You will guard him and keep him in perfect and constant peace whose mind [both its inclination and its character] is stayed on You, because he commits himself to You, leans on You, and hopes confidently in You. — Amp

People with their minds set on you, you keep completely whole. — Message

A purpose sustained thou will guard, [saying] Prosper! Prosper! Because in Thee hath he been led to trust. — Rhm

A nation of firm purpose you keep in peace; in peace, for its trust in you. — NAB

Thou dost keep in peace men of constant mind, in peace because they trust in Thee. — NEB

I decree I am setting my mind on Jesus. I decree I am leaning on Him, and confidently putting my hope in His promises. I decree He is guarding me and keeping my mind in perfect peace. I decree I am trusting God with all my heart, and He keeps me completely whole!

March 25 – Spirit Of Adoption

For ye have not received the spirit of bondage again to fear; but ye have received the Spirit of adoption, whereby we cry, Abba, Father. Romans 8:15

For [the Spirit which] you have now received [is] not a spirit of slavery to put you once more in bondage to fear, but you have received the Spirit of adoption [the Spirit producing sonship] in [the bliss of] which we cry, Abba (Father)! Father! — Amp

This resurrection life you received from God is not a timid, grave-tending life. It's adventurously expectant, greeting God with a childlike "What's next, Papa?" — Message

...a spirit of servitude leading back into fear, but ye have received a spirit of sonship. — Rhm

For you did not receive the spirit of a slave, to fill you once more with fear. — TCNT

For you have not received a Spirit of bondage, that you should go back again to the state of slavish fear... wherein we cry [unto God], saying Father. — Con

I decree I am adopted into God's family. I decree I am His son, and I am free from fear and bondage. I decree I am excited about my new adventure with Father God.

March 26 – No Doubt Here

For verily I say unto you, that whosoever shall say unto this mountain, Be thou removed, and be thou cast into the sea; and shall not doubt in his heart, but shall believe that those things which he saith shall come to pass; he shall have whatsoever he saith. Mark 11:23

Truly I tell you, whoever says to this mountain, be lifted up and thrown into the sea! And does not doubt at all in his heart but believes that what he says will take place, it will be done for him. — Amp

Embrace this God-life. Really embrace it, and nothing will be too much for you. This mountain, for instance: Just say, 'Go jump in the lake' - no shuffling or shilly-shallying - and it's as good as done. — Message

...whosoever says to this mountain and does not doubt but believes that what he says will come to pass, it will be done for him. — RSV

I decree I am confident. I decree I am not doubting in my heart that when I speak with boldness to my contrary situations, they will be changed and move. I decree I believe that I am receiving my desired end now. I decree God has already done it for me.

March 27 – Greater Works

Verily, verily, I say unto you, He that believeth on Me, the works that I do shall he do also; and greater works than these shall he do; because I go unto My Father. John 14:14

[Yes] I will grant [I Myself will do for you] whatever you shall ask in My Name [as presenting all that I AM]. —. Amp

The person who trusts Me will not only do what I am doing but even greater things, because I, on My way to the Father, am giving you the same work to do that I've been doing. — Message

...he who trusts in Me... — Mon

...will do the very deeds I do... — Mof

...and he shall do greater deeds than these... — Wey

...and he will do even greater things than these... — Phi

I decree I am trusting Jesus. I decree I am doing greater works than He did while He walked on this earth. I decree I believe Jesus gave me the power to do the greater works.

March 28 – Renewed Strength

But they that wait upon the Lord shall renew their strength; they shall mount up with wings as eagles; they shall run and not be weary; and they shall walk and not faint. Isaiah 40:31

But those who wait for the Lord [who expect, look for and hope in Him] shall change and renew their strength and power; they shall lift their wings and mount up [close to God] as eagles [mount up to the sun]; they shall run and not be weary, they shall walk and not faint or become tired. — Amp

But those who wait upon God get fresh strength. They spread their wings and soar like eagles, They run and do not get tired, they walk and do not lag behind. — Message

But those who look to the Lord will win new strength, they will run and not be weary, they will march on and never grow faint. — NEB

...they put out wings on strong pinion like eagles... — Rhm

I decree I am full of hope as I expectantly wait on the Lord. I decree I am receiving His power and strength. I decree I am walking, and I am not faint. I decree I am running, and I am not weary. I decree I am soaring like the eagles as I draw close to Father God.

March 29 – Comforting Words

This is my comfort in my affliction: for Thy word hath quickened me. Psalm 119:50b

That Your word has revived me and given me life. — Amp

These words hold me up in bad times; yes, your promises rejuvenate me. — Message

This is my comfort in my suffering. That Thy word giveth me life. — DeW

My comfort in my affliction is that your promise gives me life. — NAB

They give me strength in all my troubles; how they refresh and revive me! — Tay

I decree I am walking in God's promises. I decree His Word rejuvenates me and gives me strength. I decree His Word encourages me and revives me in times of affliction.

March 30 – Forgive And Be Forgiven

And when ye stand praying, forgive, if ye have ought against any; that your Father also which is in heaven may forgive you your trespasses. Mark 11:25

And whenever you stand praying, if you have anything against anyone, forgive him and let it drop [leave it, let it go), in order that your Father Who is in heaven may also forgive you your [own] failings and shortcomings and let them drop. — Amp

And when you assume the posture of prayer, remember that it's not all asking. If you have anything against someone, forgive - only then will your heavenly Father be inclined to also wipe your slate clean of sins. — Message

...forgive whatever wrong any man has done you. — Knox

...you must forgive anything that you are holding against anyone else and your Heavenly Father will forgive you your sins. — Phi

I decree I am forgiving those who have offended me, hurt me, or said negative things about me. I decree I release them now. Father, I ask you to forgive me of my shortcomings and mistakes and wipe my slate clean of sins.

March 31 – Let Peace Rule

And let the peace of God rule in your hearts, to the which also ye are called in one body; and be ye thankful. Colossians 3:15

And let the peace (soul harmony which comes) from Christ rule (act as umpire continually) in your hearts [deciding and settling with finality all questions that arise in your minds, in that peaceful state] to which as [members of Christ's] one body you were also called [to live]. And be thankful (appreciative), [giving praise to God always]. — Amp

Let the peace of God keep you in tune with each other, in step with each other. None of this going off and doing your own thing. And cultivate thankfulness. — Message

Let the peace that the Christ gives decide all doubts within your hearts for you also were called to the enjoyment of peace as members of one Body and show yourselves thankful. — TCNT

I decree I am praising God for His peace that rules in my heart. I decree I am letting His peace rule and reign in my life as I walk in harmony with others and cultivate a heart of thankfulness.

APRIL

*See! The
winter
is past;
the rains
are over
and gone.
Flowers
appear on
the earth;
the
season
of singing
has come,
the
cooing
of doves
is heard
in our land.
Song of Solomon 2:11-12*

April 1 – Strong And Courageous

Have I not commanded thee? Be strong and a good courage; be not afraid, neither be though dismayed: for the Lord thy God is with thee whithersoever thou goest. Joshua 1:9

Have I not commanded you? Be strong, vigorous, and very courageous. Be not afraid, neither be dismayed, for the Lord your God is with you wherever you go. — Amp

Haven't I commanded you? Strength! Courage! Do not be timid; do not get discouraged. God, your God, is with you every step you take. — Message

These are My orders: be firm and brave, never be daunted or dismayed... — Mof

...be firm and bold... — Rhm

...be fearless then, be confident... — Jerus

I decree I am living my life confidently and full of courage. I decree I know God is with me every step I take. I decree wherever I go, whatever I am doing, I am not timid or afraid. I decree I am living a bold, fearless, and courageous life.

April 2 – Praise The Lord

Praise ye the Lord. Praise God in His sanctuary: praise Him in the firmament of His power. Praise Him for His mighty acts: praise Him according to His excellent greatness. Psalm 150:1-2

Praise the Lord! Praise God in His sanctuary; praise Him in the heavens of His power! Praise Him for His mighty acts; praise Him according to the abundance of His greatness! — Amp

Hallelujah! Praise God in His holy house of worship, praise Him under the open skies; Praise Him for His acts of power, praise Him for His magnificent greatness. — Message

Hallelujah! Praise God in His sanctuary! May God be praised. Give praise to God in His shrine, glorify Him in His majestic heaven. — Har

Alleluia! Praise God in His Temple on earth, praise Him in His temple in heaven. Praise Him for high mighty achievements, praise Him for His transcendent greatness. — Jerus

I decree I am praising the Lord continually! I decree I praise Him for His magnificent greatness. I decree He is worthy of all my praise. I decree I am praising Him for His mighty acts of power displayed in my life. Hallelujah!

April 3 – Abiding Words

If ye abide in Me, and My words abide in you, ye shall ask what ye will, and it shall be done unto you. John 15:7

If you live in Me [abide vitally united to Me] and My words remain in you and continue to live in your hearts, ask whatever you will, and it shall be done for you. — Amp

But if you make yourself at home with Me and My words are at home in you, you can be sure that whatever you ask will be listened to and acted upon. — Message

If you remain in union with Me and My words remain in you, you may ask whatever you please and you shall have it. — Wms

I decree I am living and abiding in God's Word, and it is alive in my heart. Therefore, I decree I am asking God for whatever I desire of Him. I decree He is doing it for me or giving it to me because He hears me.

April 4 – Not My Words But His

Believest thou not that I am in the Father, and the Father in Me? The words that I speak unto you I speak not of Myself: but the Father that dwelleth in me he doeth the works. John 14:10

Do you not believe that I am in the Father, and that the Father is in Me? What I am telling you I do not say on My own authority and of My own accord; but the Father Who lives continually in Me does the (His) works (His own miracles, deeds of power). — Amp

Believe Me: I am in My Father and My Father is in Me. If you cannot believe that, believe what you see - these works. The person who trusts Me will not only do what I am doing but even greater things because I, on My way to the Father; am giving you the same work to do that I've been doing. — Message

...I do not speak on My own authority... — RSV

...the words I speak to you are not My own words... — Knox

I decree I am in Father God, and He, Jesus, and Holy Spirit are in me. I decree I am trusting Jesus and speaking the words He is speaking to me. I decree I do the same works today that Father God did through Jesus when He walked the earth.

April 5 – My Comforter

And I will pray the Father, and He shall give you another Comforter, that He may abide with you forever. John 14:16

And I will ask the Father, and He will give you another Comforter (Counselor, Helper, Intercessor, Advocate, Strengthener, and Standby), that He may remain with you forever. — Amp

I will talk to the Father, and He'll provide you another Friend so that you will always have someone with you. — Message

...to give you another Helper... — Mof

...another Advocate... — ABUV

...Counselor... — RSV

...another to befriend you. — Knox

...to be with you always. — Gspd

...to remain with you to the end of the age. — Wms

I decree Holy Spirit lives on the inside of me. I decree He is my Comforter, Counselor, Intercessor, Advocate, Helper, Strengthener, and Standby. I decree He is always with me and will never leave me.

April 6 – Joy Of My Heart

Thy words are found, and I did eat them; and Thy word was unto me the joy and rejoicing of mine heart; for I am called by Thy name, O Lord God of hosts. Jeremiah 15:16

Your words were found, and I ate them; and Your words were to me a joy and the rejoicing of my heart, for I am called by Your name, O Lord God of hosts. — Amp

When your words showed up, I ate them - swallowed them whole. What a feat! What delight I took in being yours, O God, God-of-the-Angel-Armies! — Message

To me Your word is a joy, making my heart glad; for I am named by Your name, O Lord God of armies. — BAS

When your words came, I devoured them; your word was my delight and the joy of my heart; for I was called by your name, Yahweh, God of Sabaoth. — Jerus

I decree I am devouring God's Word as if I were at a great feast. I decree they bring me great joy and delight in my heart. I decree I am rejoicing in my heart because God has called me by name, and I am His. Hallelujah!

April 7 – Deliverance From Evil

And the Lord shall deliver me from every evil work, and will preserve me unto His heavenly kingdom: to whom be glory for ever and ever. Amen. 2 Timothy 4:18

[And indeed] the Lord will certainly deliver and draw me to Himself from every assault of evil. He will preserve and bring me safe unto His heavenly kingdom. To Him be the glory forever and ever. Amen. — Amp

I was snatched from the jaws of the lion! God's looking after me, keeping me safe in the kingdom of heaven. All praise to Him, praise forever! Oh! Yes! — Message

...will keep me safe from ... and will give me salvation in His kingdom in heaven ... so be it! — Bas

...from every assault of evil, He will bring me safe to His own realm in heaven... — Mof

...from every attempt to do me harm, and keep me safe until His heavenly reign begins... — NEB

I decree Jesus is my Deliverer and He is drawing me to Himself. I decree He delivers me and protects me from every assault of the enemy. I decree He is preserving me forever.

April 8 – Wealth And Riches

Wealth and riches shall be in his house: and his righteousness endureth forever. Psalm 112:3

Prosperity and welfare are in his house, and his righteousness endures forever. — Amp

And the homes of the upright - how blessed! Their houses brim with wealth and a generosity that never runs dry. — Message

There will be riches and wealth for his family, and his righteousness can never change. — Jerus

Wealth and riches shall be in his house; his generosity shall endure forever. — NAB

Wealth and riches are in his house; his good fortune is unfailing. — Har

I decree I am prospering every day in every way. I decree wealth and riches are in my house continually because I am the righteousness of God. I decree I lack no good thing.

April 9 – Firmly Planted

Rooted and built up in Him, and stablished in the faith, as ye have been taught, abounding therein with thanksgiving. Colossians 2:7

Have the roots [of your being] firmly and deeply planted [in Him, fixed and founded in Him], being continually built up in Him, becoming increasingly more confirmed and established in the faith, just as you were taught, and abounding and overflowing in it with thanksgiving. — Amp

You're deeply rooted in Him. You're well constructed upon Him. You know your way around the faith. Now do what you've been taught. School's out; quit studying the subject and start living it! And let your living spill over into thanksgiving. — Message

Having the roots of your being firmly planted in Him, and continually building yourselves up in Him, and always being increasingly confirmed in the faith. — Wey

I decree I am firmly rooted and grounded in Jesus. I decree my faith is built up in Him. I decree it is established and increasing daily. I decree I continually abound and overflow with thanksgiving.

April 10 – God Is For Me

What shall we then say to these things? If God be for us, who can be against us? Romans 8:31

What then shall we say to [all] this? If God is for us, who [can be] against us? [Who can be our foe, if God is on our side?]. — Amp

With God on our side like this, how can we lose? — Message

Then what shall we conclude from this... — Gspd

In face of all this, what is there left to say... — Phi

If God is on our side, who can there be against us... — TCNT

Just this - if God is for us, what does it matter who may be against us... — Nor

I decree I am on God's side, and He is for me. I decree it does not matter who comes against me, I cannot lose because He made me a winner.

April 11 – Overcoming Victory

He that overcometh shall inherit all things; and I will be his God, and he shall be My son. Revelation 21:7

He who is victorious shall inherit all these things, and I will be God to him and he shall be My son. — Amp

Conquerors inherit all this. I'll be God to them, they'll be sons and daughters to Me. — Message

...shall inherit these things... — ASV

The victory shall inherit all this... — Ber

All this is the victor's heritage... — NEB

I decree I am inheriting all of God's blessings because I am an over-comer. I decree God is my God, and I am His son. I decree He has made me more than a conqueror and I am victorious.

April 12 – Be At Peace

Acquaint now thyself with Him, and be at peace: thereby good shall come unto thee. Job 22:21

Acquaint now yourself with Him [agree with God and show yourself to be conformed to His will] and be at peace; by that [you shall prosper and great] good shall come to you. — Amp

Give in to God, come to terms with Him and everything will turn out just fine. — Message

Well then! Make peace with Him, be reconciled and all your happiness will be restored to you. — Jerus

Shew thyself to be one with Him - I pray thee - and prosper, thereby shall there come on thee blessing. — Rhm

Come to terms with God and you will prosper, that is the way to mend your fortune. — NEB

...thereby thine increase is good. — YLT

I decree I am conforming myself to God's will for my life and I am at peace. I decree everything is going to be fine for me. I decree I am prospering, and my happiness is being restored. I decree good things are coming to me now.

April 13 – In His Love

If ye keep My commandments, ye shall abide in My love; even as I have kept My Father's commandments, and abide in His love. John 15:10

If you keep My commandments [if you continue to obey My instructions] you will abide in My love and live on in it, just as I have obeyed My Father's commandments and live on in His love. — Amp

If you keep My commands, you'll remain intimately at home in My love. That's what I've done - kept My Father's commands and made Myself at home in His love. — Message

If you continue to keep My commands, you will remain in My love, just as I have kept My Father's commands and remain in His love. — Wms

I decree I am keeping God's commands and instructions just as Jesus kept His Father's commands. I decree I am abiding and remaining in God's love just as Jesus abode in His Father's love.

April 14 – Only Believe

As soon as Jesus heard the word that was spoken, He saith unto the ruler of the synagogue, be not afraid, only believe. Mark 5:36

Overhearing but ignoring what they said, Jesus said to the ruler of the synagogue, do not be seized with alarm and struck with fear; only keep on believing. — Amp

Jesus overheard what they were talking about and said to the leader, "Do not listen to them; just trust Me." — Message

But Jesus paid no attention to what was said... — Wms

Jesus heard them say this but took no notice... — Rieu

Fear not... — ASV

Have no fear, only believe! — Ber

Now do not be afraid, just go on believing! — Phi

I decree I am believing God's Word and I am not in fear. I decree I am not moved by situations around me that are trying to hinder me. I decree I am putting my trust in God, and I keep believing.

April 15 – All Profit

Moreover the profit of the earth is for all... Ecclesiastes 5:9a

Moreover, the profit of the earth is for all... — Amp

But the good earth does not cheat anyone... — Message

And the abundance of the land is for all... — YLT

I decree I am believing that I am receiving all the abundance of the land today. I decree today is my harvest day and I will profit from it. I decree it is mine now and I receive it in the authority of the Name of Jesus.

April 16 – Greater Works

Verily, verily, I say unto you, he that believeth on Me, the works that I do shall he do also; and greater works than these shall he do; because I go unto My Father. John 14:12

I assure you, most solemnly I tell you, if anyone steadfastly believes in Me, he will himself be able to do the things that I do; and he will do even greater things than these, because I go to the Father. — Amp

The person who trusts Me will not only do what I am doing but even greater things, because I, on My way to the Father, am giving you the same work to do that I've been doing. — Message

...whoever perseveres in believing in Me, can himself do the things that I am doing... — Wms

...will do the very deed I do... — Mof

...and he shall do greater deeds than these... — Wey

I decree I am believing in Jesus and trusting in the power of Holy Spirit that dwells in me. I decree I am doing the same works and even greater works than Jesus did because He went to His Father.

April 17 – God Loves Me

Herein is love, not that we loved God, but that He loved us, and sent His Son to be the propitiation for our sins. 1 John 4:10

In this is love; and not that we loved God, but that He loved us and sent His Son to be the propitiation (the atoning sacrifice) for our sins. — Amp

Not that we once upon a time loved God, but that He loved us and sent His Son as a sacrifice to clear away our sins and the damage they've done to our relationship with God. — Message

Love lies in this, not in our love for God but in His love for us. — Mof

The love consists not in our having loved God, but in His loving us and sending His Son as an atoning sacrifice for our sins. — Gspd

In this is love, not that we loved God but that He loved us and sent His Son to be the expiation for our sins. — RSV

...to make personal atonement for ... — Phi

I decree I am loving God because He loves me. I decree He sent His Son as a sacrifice for me so I can be forgiven of my sins and have a relationship with Father God.

April 18 – The Greatest Is Love

And now abideth faith, hope, charity, these three; but the greatest of these is charity. 1 Corinthians 13:13

And so faith, hope, love, abide [faith-conviction and belief respecting man's relation to God and divine thing; hope - joyful and confident expectation of eternal salvation: love - true affection for God and man, growing out of God 's love for and in us], these three; but the greatest of these is love. — Amp

But for right now, until that completeness, we have three things to do to lead us toward that consummation: trust steadily in God, hope unswervingly, love extravagantly. And the best of the three is love. — Message

There are three things - faith, hope, love - that keep on forever. — Tay

...but the most important of these is love. — Beck

I decree I am faithfully putting my trust in God. I decree my hope in Him is unwavering. I decree I am walking in an extravagant love toward God and my fellow man.

April 19 – Draw From The Well

Therefore with joy shall ye draw water out of the wells of salvation. Isaiah 12:3

Therefore with joy will you draw water from the wells of salvation. — Amp

Joyfully you'll pull up buckets of water from the wells of salvation. — Message

Therefore shall ye draw water with rejoicing, out of the fountains. —Rhm

Even with triumphant joy shall ye draw waters from the fountain. —Sprl

Joyfully then shall you draw upon the fountains of deliverance. — Mof

So rejoicing you shall drink deep from the fountain of deliverance. — Knox

I decree I am stirring up the gift of joy within me. I decree I am drinking from the wells of salvation, the living water, and I have a continual feast in God's presence.

April 20 – Choose Life

I call heaven and earth to record this day against you, that I have set before you life and death, blessing and cursing: therefore choose life, that both them and thy seed may live.
Deuteronomy 30:19

I call heaven and earth to witness this day against you that I have set before you life and death, the blessings and the curses; therefore, choose life, that you and your descendants may live. — Amp

I place before you life and death, blessing and curse. Choose life so that you and your children will live. — Message

...the blessing and the curse... — ASV

...that you and your descendants may live. — RSV

I decree I am choosing life and blessing today. I decree I am walking in the abundant life God has prepared for me. I decree my children, as well as my children's, children's children, are fully blessed because I choose life.

April 21 – Exceeding Abundantly

Now unto Him that is able to do exceeding abundantly above all that we ask or think, according to the power that worketh in us. Ephesians 3:20

Now to Him Who, by (in consequence of) the [action of His] power that is at work within us, is able to [carry out His purpose and] do super-abundantly, far over and above all that we [dare] ask or think [infinitely beyond our highest prayers, desires, thoughts, hopes or dreams]. — Amp

God can do anything, you know - far more than you could ever imagine or guess or request in your wildest dreams! He does it not by pushing us around but by working within us, His Spirit deeply and gently within us. — Message

...able to do far more than anything that we can ask or conceive through the power which is at work with us. — TCNT

I decree God's energizing power is working within me doing exceedingly abundantly above anything I could ask or think or imagine. I decree He is exceeding my wildest dreams by Holy Spirit working inside me.

April 22 –Protected By God

We know that whosoever is born of God sinneth not; but he that is begotten of God keepeth himself, and that wicked one toucheth him not.
1 John 5:18

We know [absolutely] that anyone born of God does not [deliberately and knowingly] practice committing sin, but the One Who was begotten of God carefully watches over and protects him [Christ's divine presence within him preserves him against the evil], and the wicked one does not lay hold (get a grip) on him or touch [him]. — Amp

We know that none of the God-begotten makes a practice of sin - fatal sin. The God-begotten are also the God-protected. The Evil One cannot lay a hand on them. — Message

...that no one who has received the new Life from God lives in sin... — TCNT

I decree I belong to God. I decree I do not deliberately or knowingly practice committing sin. I decree Holy Spirit is in me, watching over and protecting me. I decree Jesus is preserving me against the evils of Satan, and he cannot touch me.

April 23 – Sons Of God

For as many as are led by the Spirit of God, they are the sons of God. Romans 8:14

For all who are led by the Spirit of God are sons of God. — Amp

God's Spirit beckons. There are things to do and places to go! — Message

For all who are led by God's Spirit, and they alone, are the sons of God. — Con

For only those are sons of God who are led by God's Spirit. — Mon

Those who follow the leading of God's Spirit are all God's sons. — Knox

I decree I am being led by Holy Spirit and God calls me His son. I decree He leads me; therefore, I belong to Him. I decree I am God's favorite child. I decree I have things to do for God and places He wants me to go.

April 24 – Heirs By Faith

For the promise, that he should be the heir of the world, was not to Abraham, or to his seed, through the law, but through the righteousness of faith. Romans 4:13

For the promise of Abraham or his posterity, that he should inherit the world, did not come through [observing the commands of] the Law but through the righteousness of faith. — Amp

That famous promise God gave Abraham - that he and his children would possess the earth - was not given because of something Abraham did or would do. It was based on God's decision to put everything together for him, which Abraham then entered when he believed. — Message

The promise made to Abraham and his descendants - that they should possess the earth - was given, not because of their keeping the law but because of justification by faith. — Nor

I decree I am living in all the promises God gave to Abraham because I am living by faith. I decree I am the righteousness of God through Jesus Christ and not of my own works. I decree my faith qualified me to receive all of God's blessings.

April 25 – Mercy Forever

O give thanks unto the Lord; for He is good: because His mercy endureth forever. Psalm 118:1

O Give thanks to the Lord, for He is good; for His mercy and loving kindness endure forever! — Amp

Thank God because He's good, because His love never quits. — Message

O give thanks unto the Lord, for He is gracious. — PBV

...for His lovingkindness endureth for ever. — ASV

...His love is everlasting! — Jerus

...His steadfast love endures for ever! — RSV

...His kindness never fails. — Mof

I decree I am thanking my Lord, Jesus, every day. I decree His goodness and mercy toward me endure forever. I decree His love for me never quits.

April 26 – I Believe I Receive

Therefore I say unto you, whatsoever things ye desire, when ye pray, believe that ye receive them, and ye shall have them. Mark 11:24

For this reason I am telling you, whatever you ask for in prayer, believe (trust and be confident) that it is granted to you, and you will [get it]. — Amp

...it's as good as done... — Message

...whatsoever you pray about and ask for... — Phi

...whatever you ask in prayer... — RSV

...you will receive it. — Nor

...ye have received. — Alf

...and it will be yours. — NEB

I decree when I pray, I trust God to answer me. I decree I have the confidence to believe I receive the things I pray for. I decree I have them now, so I am celebrating now. I decree I am calling it done and rejoice in the victory!

April 27 – Faithful To Forgive

If we confess our sins, He is faithful and just to forgive us our sins, and to cleanse us from all unrighteousness. 1 John 1:9

If we [freely] admit that we have sinned and confess our sins, He is faithful and just (true to His own nature and promises) and will forgive our sins [dismiss our lawlessness] and [continuously] cleanse us from all unrighteousness [everything not in conformity to His will in purpose, thought and action]. — Amp

On the other hand, if we admit our sins - make a clean breast of them - He won't let us down; He'll be true to Himself. He'll forgive our sins and purge us of all wrongdoing. — Message

If we acknowledge our sins He is upright and can be depended on to forgive us our sins to cleanse us from everything wrong. — Gspd

I decree I am confessing any sin that hinders my relationship with Father God. I decree He is faithful to forgive me and cleanse me from all unrighteousness so I can conform to His purpose, thoughts, and actions.

April 28 – Clean And Humble

Therefore, lay apart all filthiness and superfluity of naughtiness, and receive with meekness the engrafted word, which is able to save your souls. James 1:21

So get rid of all uncleanness and the rampant outgrowth of wickedness and in a humble (gentle, modest) spirit receive and welcome the Word which implanted and rooted [in your hearts] contains the power to save your souls. — Amp

So throw all spoiled virtue and cancerous evil in the garbage. In simple humility, let our gardener, God, landscape you with the Word, making a salvation-garden of your life. — Message

Therefore, have done with all filthiness and whatever wickedness still remains and in a humble spirit receive that Message which has been implanted in your hearts. — TCNT

I decree I am humbling myself before Father God and getting rid of all uncleanness in my heart. I decree I am preparing my heart to receive His Word that saves me, delivers me, and sets me free.

April 29 – Rejoice In Hope

By whom also we have access by faith into this grace wherein we stand, and rejoice in hope of the glory of God. Romans 5:2

Through Him also we have [our] access (entrance, introduction) by faith into this grace (state of God's favor) in which we [firmly and safely] stand. And let us rejoice and exult in our hope of experiencing and enjoying the glory of God. — Amp

We throw open our doors to God and discover at the same moment that He has already thrown open His door to us. We find ourselves standing where we always hoped we might stand-out in the wide open spaces of God's grace and glory, standing tall and shouting our praises. — Message

Through whom also we have had our introduction by our faith into this favour wherein we stand... — Rhm

...and triumph in the hope of God's glory. — Mof

I decree I am entering into God's grace by faith. I decree I am standing firm in His favor. I decree I am rejoicing in God's glory and His goodness while I become all that He created me to be.

April 30 – Blessed With Abraham

So then they which be of faith are blessed with faithful Abraham. Galatians 3:9

So then, those who are people of faith are blessed and made happy and favored by God [as partners in fellowship] with the believing and trusting Abraham. — Amp

So those now who lived by faith are blessed along with Abraham, who lived by faith - this is no new doctrine. — Message

So we see that those who rest on faith are blessed with believing Abraham. — Wey

So then those who are of faith have a part in the blessing of Abraham who was full of faith. — Bas

So those who believe are blessed with Abraham, who believed. — Beck

I decree I am living my life full of faith. I decree I am talking faith and walking in faith. I decree I am blessed, happy, and favored by God. I decree I am enjoying the same blessings Abraham receive because he lived by faith.

MAY

How good
You are
to me!
When people
turn to
You,
Yahweh,
they
discover how
easy You
are to
please—
so faithful
and true!
Joyfully You
teach them the
proper path,
even when
they go
astray.
Psalm 25:8

May 1 – Faith Conquers

For whatsoever is born of God overcometh the world: and this is the victory that overcometh the world, even our faith. 1 John 5:4

For whatever is born of God is victorious over the world; and this is the victory that conquers the world, even our faith. — Amp

Every God-begotten person conquers the world's ways. The conquering power that brings the world to its knees is our faith. — Message

Because all that has received new life from God conquers the world, and this is the power that has conquered the world - our faith! — TCNT

The victory that defeats the world is our faith. — NEB

I decree I am born of God. I decree His Holy Spirit lives in me. I decree my faith is what defeats the world. I decree it is making me a victorious conqueror over the world.

May 2 – God's Heir

Wherefore thou art no more a servant, but a son; and if a son, then an heir of God through Christ. Galatians 4:7

Therefore, you are no longer a slave (bond servant) but a son; and if a son, then [it follows that you are] an heir by the aid of God, through Christ. — Amp

Doesn't that privilege of intimate conversation with God make it plain, that you are not a slave, but a child? And if you are a child, you're also an heir, with complete access to the inheritance. — Message

So you are no longer a slave, but a son; and if a son, then an heir, made so by God. — Gspd

I decree I am God's child, and I am no longer a slave to this world. I decree I am an heir to His inheritance through Christ Jesus. I decree I have the privilege of intimate conversations with God. Therefore, I believe I receive all God has for me today.

May 3 – Saving Faith

And he said to the woman, thy faith hath saved thee; go in peace. Luke 7:50

But Jesus said to the woman. Your faith has saved you; go (enter) into peace [in freedom from all the distresses that are experienced as the result of sin]. — Amp

He ignored them and said to the woman, "Your faith has saved you. Go in peace." — Message

...by your faith you have salvation... — Bas

...it is your faith which has saved you... — Gspd

I decree my faith in Jesus has saved me. I decree I am entering into His peace and reside there. I decree He gives me freedom from all the distresses I am experiencing as a result of sin, or wrong choices.

May 4 – Reigning On The Earth

And hast made us unto our God kings and priests: and we shall reign on the earth. Revelation 5:10

And You have made them a kingdom (royal race) and priests to our God, and they shall reign [as kings] over the earth! — Amp

Then you make them a Kingdom, Priests for our God, Priest-kings to rule over the earth. — Message

And madest them to be unto our God a kingdom and priests; and they reign... — ASV

And did make them a Kingdom of Priests in the service of our God, and they are reigning upon the earth. — TCNT

Thou has made us a royal race of priests, to serve God; we shall reign as kings over the earth. — Knox

I decree God has made me a royal race of priests to serve Him. I decree I am ruling and reigning over the enemy as a king in my domain in Jesus' name.

May 5 – Ask For Wisdom

If any of you lack wisdom, let him ask of God, that giveth to all men liberally, and upbraideth not; and it shall be given him. James 1:5

If any of you is deficient in wisdom, let him ask of the giving God [Who gives] to everyone liberally and ungrudgingly, without reproaching or faultfinding, and it will be given him. — Amp

If you do not know what you're doing, pray to the Father. He loves to help. You'll get His help, and won't be condescended to when you ask for it. — Message

But if any of you is coming short of wisdom... — Rhm

...who gives freely to everyone without reproaches... — TCNT

...who gives generously and does not reproach one with it afterwards... — Gspd

...who gives with open hand... — Wey

I decree I am walking in Divine wisdom. I decree God gives me a generous supply of wisdom when I ask for it because He loves to help me. I decree He does not make me feel bad for asking for more wisdom.

May 6 – Spiritually Minded

For to be carnally minded is death; but to be spiritually minded is life and peace. Romans 8:6

Now the mind of the flesh [which is sense and reason without the Holy Spirit] is death [death that comprises all the miseries arising from sin, both here and hereafter]. But the mind of the [Holy] Spirit is life and [soul] peace [both now and forever]. — Amp

Those who trust God's action in them find that God's Spirit is in them - living and breathing God! — Message

The interests of the flesh mean death, the interests of the Spirit mean life and peace. — Mof

For the mind of the flesh is death; but the mind of the Spirit is life and peace. — ASV

But to set the mind on the flesh brings death, whereas to set the mind on the Spirit brings life and peace. — Nor

I decree I am setting my mind on the things of the Spirit realm. I decree I am not focusing on things of the earthly realm. I decree I am full of life and my mind is full of peace.

May 7 – Reap In Joy

They that sow in tears shall reap in joy. Psalm 126:5

They who sow in tears shall reap in joy and singing. — Amp

So those who planted their crops in despair will shout hurrahs at the harvest. — Message

They who are sowing with tears with shouting shall reap. — Rhm

Let them who sow with tears reap with rapture. — Sept

May those who sow in tears reap with shouts of joy! — AAT

I decree I may be sowing my seeds in tears, but Hallelujah! I decree I will reap my harvest with shouts of joy rejoicing in the goodness of the Lord!

May 8 – Justified By Faith

Therefore we conclude that a man is justified by faith without the deeds of the law. Romans 3:28

For we hold that a man is justified and made upright by faith independent of and distinctly apart from good deeds (works of the Law). [The observance of the Law had nothing to do with justification.]. — Amp

What we've learned is this: God does not respond to what we do, we respond to what God does. We've finally figured it out. — Message

For we conclude that a man is pronounced righteous on the ground of faith, quite apart from the obedience of Law. — TCNT

For we hold that a man is brought into right standing with God by faith, that observance of the law has no connection with it. — Wms

So it is that we are saved by faith in Christ and not by the good things we do. — Tay

I decree I am righteous, in right standing with God, because of my faith in Christ Jesus, not by my works or the Law. I decree God does not respond to what I do. I decree I respond to what He does.

May 9 – The Love Of Christ

Who shall separate us from the love of Christ? Shall tribulation, or distress, or persecution, or famine, or nakedness, or peril, or sword? Romans 8:35

Who shall ever separate us from Christ's love? Shall suffering and affliction and tribulation? Or calamity and distress? Or persecution or hunger or destitution or peril or sword? — Amp

Do you think anyone is going to be able to drive a wedge between us and Christ's love for us? There is no way! Not trouble, not hard times, not hatred, not hunger, not homelessness, not bullying threats, not backstabbing. — Message

Who can separate us...can suffering, or straightness of distress, or persecution, or famine, or nakedness or the peril of our lives, or the swords of our enemies? — Con

I decree there is nothing that I go through that can separate me from the love of Christ Jesus. I decree He loves me so much and I am His favorite child.

May 10 – God Hears Me

In my distress I called upon the Lord, and cried unto my God: He heard my voice out of His temple, and my cry came before Him, even into His ears. Psalm 18:6

In my distress [when seemingly closed in] I called upon the Lord and cried to my God; He heard my voice out of His temple (heavenly dwelling place), and my cry came before Him, and His [very] ears. — Amp

A hostile world! I call to God, I cry to God to help me. From His palace He hears my call; my cry brings me right into His presence - a private audience! — Message

Then in anguish of heart I cried to the Lord, I called for help to my God... — NEB

He heard out of His temple my voice, and my outcry for help came before Him - entered into His ears! — Rhm

I decree I have a personal audience with Father God all the time. I decree when I cry out to Him for help, He always hears my voice. I decree my prayers bring me right into His presence since He hears me.

May 11 – Sing God's Praises

I will praise Thee, O Lord, among the people: and I will sing praises unto Thee among the nations. Psalm 108:3

I will praise and give thanks to You, O Lord, among the peoples; and I will sing praises unto You among the nations. — Amp

I am thanking you, God, out in the streets, singing your praises in town and country. — Message

I will give thanks unto Thee, O Jehovah, among the peoples; and I will sing praises unto Thee among the nations. — ASV

I decree I am singing God's highest praises everywhere I go, across all the nations. I decree I am telling everyone of His goodness and thanking Him for all He does for me.

May 12 – Grace To Be Rich

For ye know the grace of our Lord Jesus Christ, that though He was rich, yet for your sakes He became poor, that ye through His poverty might be rich. **2 Corinthians 8:9**

For you are becoming progressively acquainted with and recognizing more strongly and clearly the grace of our Lord Jesus Christ (His kindness, His gracious generosity, His undeserved favor and spiritual blessing), [in] that though He was [so very] rich, yet for your sakes He became [so very] poor, in order that by His poverty you might become enriched (abundantly supplied). — Amp

Rich as He was, He gave it all away for us - in one stroke He became poor and we became rich. — Message

You know how gracious our Lord Jesus Christ was; rich though He was, He became poor for the sake of you, that by His poverty you might be rich. — Mof

I decree I am progressively becoming acquainted with and recognizing more strongly and clearly the grace of our Lord Jesus Christ. I decree He took my poverty so I can be rich. I decree today I walk in His grace and anointing for overflowing prosperity and abundance.

May 13 – Head And Not The Tail

And the Lord shall make thee the head, and not the tail; and thou shalt be above only, and thou shalt not be beneath; if that thou hearken unto the commandments of the Lord thy God, which I command thee this day, to observe and to do them. Deuteronomy 28:13

And the Lord shall make you the head, and not the tail; and you shall be above only, and you shall not be beneath, if you heed the commandments of the Lord your God which I command you this day and are watchful to do them. — Amp

God will make you the head, not the tail; you'll always be the top dog, never the bottom dog, as you obediently listen to and diligently keep the commands of God, your God, that I am commanding you today. — Message

...you shall be always rising, never falling... — Mof

I decree I am walking in the commandment to walk in love. I decree I am the head, and I am not the tail. I decree I am above only, and never beneath. I decree I am always rising and going over. I am never falling or going under.

May 14 – Loaded Daily

Blessed be the Lord, who daily loadeth us with benefits, even the God of our salvation. Psalm 68:19

Blessed be the Lord, Who bears our burdens and carries us day by day, even the God Who is our salvation! Selah [pause, and calmly think of that]! — Amp

Blessed be the Lord - day after day He carries us along. He's our Savior, our God, oh yes! He's God-for-us, He's God who saves-us. — Message

Blessed be the Lord, who daily beareth our burden, even the God who is our salvation. — RV

Blessed be the Lord, who daily bears us up; God is our salvation. — RSV

May the Lord be blessed for sustaining us daily, the God who is our deliverance. — Har

I decree I am blessing the Lord. I decree He is bearing my burdens and carrying me every day in exchange for loading me daily with all of His benefits.

May 15 – Full Joy

Hitherto have ye asked nothing in My name: ask, and ye shall receive, that your joy may be full. John 16:24

Up to this time you have not asked a [single] thing in My Name [as presenting all that I AM]; but now ask and keep on asking and you will receive, so that your joy (gladness, delight) may be full and complete. — Amp

Ask the Father for whatever is in keeping with the things I've revealed to you. Ask in My name, according to My will, and He'll most certainly give it to you. Your joy will be a river overflowing it banks! — Message

Ask now...that your joy may be overflowing. — Phi

...so that your joy may be complete. — Nor

...to bring you gladness in full measure. — Knox

I decree I am asking Father God, in the Name of Jesus, for everything I want, need or desire. I decree they are in accordance with His will. I decree He is giving them to me, and I receive them from Him now so that I will have overflowing joy. Joy like a river.

May 16 — God's Free Gift

For the wages of sin is death; but the gift of God is eternal life through Jesus Christ our Lord. Romans 6:23

For the wages which sin pays is death, but the [bountiful] free gift of God is eternal life through (in union with) Jesus Christ our Lord. — Amp

Work for sin your whole life and your pension is death. But God's gift is real life, eternal life, delivered by Jesus, or Master. — Message

Sin pays its servants: the wage is death but God gives to those who serve Him: His free gift is eternal life through Christ Jesus our Lord. — Phi

But the gift of God is Immortal Life, through union with Christ Jesus, our Lord. — TCNT

I decree I am no longer living a life of sin which leads to death. I decree God has given me the free gift of eternal life through His son, Jesus. I decree I accept this free gift and I have eternal life through my union with Jesus Christ.

May 17 – A Better Covenant

But now hath He obtained a more excellent ministry, by how much also He is the mediator of a better covenant, which was established upon better promises. Hebrews 8:6

But as it now is, He [Christ] has acquired a [priestly] ministry which is as much superior and more excellent [than the old] as the covenant (the agreement) of which He is the Mediator (the Arbiter, Agent) is superior and more excellent, [because] it is enacted and rests upon more important (sublimer, higher, and nobler) promises. — Amp

But Jesus' priestly work far surpasses what these other priests do, since He's working from a far better plan. If the first plan - the old covenant - had worked out, a second wouldn't have been needed. — Message

As it is, however, the divine service He has obtained is superior owing to the fact that He mediates a superior covenant. — Mof

I decree I am living in a better covenant with more excellent promise because of the shed Blood of Jesus Christ. I decree Jesus is now my Mediator with a far better plan for me. I decree He is offering me His higher and nobler promises.

May 18 – Trust In The Lord

Wait on the Lord: be of good courage, and He shall strengthen thine heart: wait, I say, on the Lord. Psalm 27:14

Wait and hope for and expect the Lord; be brave and of good courage and let your heart be stout and enduring. Yes, wait for and hope for and expect the Lord. — Amp

Stay with God! Take heart. Do not quit. I'll say it again: stay with God. — Message

Wait for the Lord with courage; be stout-hearted... — NAB

Wait for Jehovah: be strong, and let thy heart take courage... — ASV

Wait thou for Yahweh. Be strong and let thy heart be bold... — Rhm

Wait patiently for the Lord, to help thee; be brave, and let thy heart take comfort... — Knox

Trust in the Lord... — Har

I decree I am staying with God. As I am waiting and hoping on the Lord with great expectancy, I decree I am strong and courageous. I decree I am trusting Him and take comfort in knowing He is helping me.

May 19 – Enter In By The Blood

Having therefore, brethren, boldness to enter into the holiest by the Blood of Jesus. Hebrews 10:19

Therefore, brethren, since we have full freedom and confidence to enter into the [Holy of] Holies [by the power and virtue] in the Blood of Jesus. — Amp

So, friends, we can now - without hesitation - walk right up to God, into "the Holy Place." Jesus has cleared the way by the Blood of His sacrifice, acting as our priest before God. The "curtain" into God's presence is His body. — Message

...boldness for the entrance into the holy places by the... — ABUV

...a cheerful confidence...to enter into the Holiest by... — Mon

...free access to the sanctuary through... — Gspd

...freedom of speech for the entrance through the Holy place by... — Rhm

I decree I am coming boldly, with a cheerful confidence, with no hesitation, right into the Holy of Holies, the Throne Room of Grace, by power of the Blood of Jesus.

May 20 – Strong, Vigorous, Victorious

...I have written unto you, young men, because ye are strong, and the word of God abideth in you, and ye have overcome the wicked one. 1 John 2:14b

...I write to you young men, because you are strong and vigorous, and the Word of God is [always] abiding in you (in your heart), and you have been victorious over the wicked one. — Amp

...and you newcomers - such vitality and strength! God's word is so steady in you. Your fellowship with God enables you to gain a victory over the Evil One. — Message

...because you are vigorous... — Ber

...is treasured in your hearts... — Nor

...you have a hold on God's truth... — Phi

...conquered the wicked one. — Wms

I decree I am strong and vigorous because the Word of God is always abiding in me. I decree I treasure God's Word and fellowship with Him on a continual basis which enables me to overcome and conquer the wicked one. I decree I am victorious over him now.

May 21 – Grow In Wisdom

And Jesus increased in wisdom and stature, and in favour with God and man. Luke 2:52

And Jesus increased in wisdom (in broad and full understanding) and in stature and years, and in favor with God and man. — Amp

And Jesus matured, growing up in both body and spirit, blessed by both God and people. — Message

And Jesus was ever advancing in wisdom and in stature. — Mon

And Jesus grew in wisdom as He grew in years and gained the blessing of God and men. — TCNT

He grew also in the love of God and of those who knew Him. — Phi

...and won the approval of God and all people. — Beck

I decree I am growing and maturing in my body as well as my spirit. I decree I am advancing in wisdom, knowledge, and understanding. I decree I am increasing in favor with God and man.

May 22 – Free From The Law Of Sin And Death

For the law of the Spirit of life in Christ Jesus hath made me free from the law of sin and death. Romans 8:2

For the law of the Spirit of life [which is] in Christ Jesus [the law of our new being] has freed me from the law of sin and of death. — Amp

The Spirit of life in Christ, like a strong wind, has magnificently cleared the air, freeing you from a fated lifetime of brutal tyranny at the hands of sin and death. — Message

For through your union with Christ Jesus, the law of the life-giving Spirit, has set you free. — TCNT

For the law of the spirit of life... — Rhm

For the new spiritual principle of life... — Phi

...lifts me out... — Phi

I decree I am living free from the Law of Sin and Death. I decree the Spirit of life which is in Christ Jesus has magnificently cleared the air and I am living free from a lifetime of brutal tyranny. I decree I am freed from bondage.

May 23 – The Power Of God

For the preaching of the cross is to them that perish foolishness; but unto us which are saved it is the power of God. 1 Corinthians 1:18

For the story and message of the cross is sheer absurdity and folly to those who are perishing and on their way to perdition, but to us who are being saved it is the [manifestation of] the power of God. — Amp

The Message that points to the Christ on the Cross seems like sheer silliness to those hell-bent on destruction, but for those on the way of salvation it makes perfect sense. — Message

The Message of the Cross is indeed mere folly to those who are in the path to Ruin, but to us who are in the path of Salvation it is the very power of God. — TCNT

Those who are doomed to perish find the story of the cross sheer folly... — Mof

...it means all the power of God. — Gspd

I decree I am receiving the power of the Cross in my life. I decree the Cross represents the power of God through Christ Jesus, my Risen Savior, and what He can do!

May 24 – Sing Unto The Lord

I will sing unto the Lord as long as I live: I will sing praise to my God while I have my being. Psalm 104:33

I will sing to the Lord as long as I live: I will sing praise to my God while I have any being. — Amp

Oh, let me sing to God, all my life long, sing hymns to my God as long as I live! — Message

I will sing to Yahweh as long as I live! Yea I will touch the strings to my God while I continue. — Rhm

I decree I am singing praises to my great God, as long as I live and have breath in my body. I decree He is so good to me. I decree I will sing His praises for who He is to me!

May 25 – Abraham's Seed

And if ye be Christ's, then are ye Abraham's seed, and heirs according to the promise. Galatians 3:29

And if you belong to Christ [are in Him Who is Abraham's Seed], then you are Abraham's offspring and [spiritual] heirs according to promise. — Amp

Also, since you are Christ's family, then you are Abraham's famous "descendant," heirs according to the covenant promises. — Message

And since you belong to Christ, it follows that you are Abraham's offspring and, under the promise, sharers in the inheritance. — TCNT

As if you belong to Christ, then you are indeed Abraham's children; the promised inheritance is yours. — Knox

But if you thus belong to Christ, you are the 'issue' of Abraham, and so heirs by promise. — NEB

I decree I am Abraham's seed because I belong to Christ Jesus who is Abraham's seed. I decree I am a spiritual heir according to the covenant promise. I decree I share the same inheritance Jesus has because God sees me as He sees Jesus.

May 26 – Knowing All Things

But ye have an unction from the Holy One, and ye know all things. 1 John 2:20

But you have been anointed by [you hold a sacred appointment from, you have been given an unction from] the Holy One, and you all know [the Truth] or you know all things. — Amp

But you belong. The Holy One anointed you, and you all know it. — Message

Besides, you hold your anointing from the Holy One... — Ber

But you have been anointed by the Holy One... — RSV

...and you all know... — RSV

...and now all of you know... — Beck

I decree I am anointed by Holy Spirit, and I belong to God. I decree I have a sacred appointment from Holy Spirit, and I have an unction in me from Him that leads me into knowing the truth in all things.

May 27 – Healing The Sick

And Jesus went about all the cities and villages, teaching in their synagogues, and preaching the gospel of the kingdom, and healing every sickness and every disease among the people. Matthew 9:35

And Jesus went about all the cities and villages, teaching in their synagogues and proclaiming the good news (the Gospel) of the kingdom and curing all kinds of disease and every weakness and infirmity. — Amp

Then Jesus made a circuit of all the towns and villages. He taught in their meeting places, reported kingdom news, and healed their diseased bodies, healed their bruised and hurt lives. — Message

...and healing all manner of disease and all manner of sickness... — ASV

I decree Jesus is my Healer. I decree He heals all my sicknesses; all my diseases and I receive everything that He shed His Blood for me to have so I can walk in victory. I decree He has already paid the price for me to be free from every weakness and infirmity in my body. I decree it is gone in Jesus' name.

May 28 – An Intimate Language

For he that speaketh in an unknown tongue speaketh not unto men, but unto God: for no man understandeth him; howbeit in the spirit he speaketh mysteries. 1 Corinthians 14:2

For one who speaks in an [unknown] tongue speaks not to men but to God, for no one understands or catches His meaning, because in the [Holy] Spirit he utters secret truths and hidden things [not obvious to the understanding]. — Amp

If you praise Him in the private language of tongues, God understands you but no one else does, for you are sharing intimacies just between you and Him. — Message

When a man is using the language of ecstacy he is talking...not with men, he is no doubt inspired, but he speaks mysteries. — NEB

When a man talks a strange language, he doesn't talk to people... — Beck

I decree I am continuously praying in my first language, my Heavenly language, or other tongues. I decree that although no one understands this language, I am speaking directly to My Heavenly Father. I decree I am praying out His divine mysteries, secret truths, and the hidden things for my life.

May 29 – Faith-Filled Words

We have the same spirit of faith, according as it is written, I believed, and therefore have I spoken; we also believe, and therefore speak. 2 Corinthians 4:13

Yet we have the same spirit of faith as he had who wrote, I have believed, and therefore have I spoken. We to believe, and therefore we speak. — Amp

We're not keeping this quiet, not on your life. Just like the psalmist who wrote, "I believed it, so I said it," we say what we believe. — Message

Yet having the same spirit of faith whereof it is written I believed, and therefore did I speak, I also believe, and therefore speak. — TCNT

But since our spirit of faith is the same; therefore - as it is written, I believed and so I spoke - I too believe and so I speak. — Mof

...speak our minds with full confidence. — Knox

I decree I have the same Spirit of Faith living in me that was in Jesus! I decree I believe I have creative power when I speak, so I speak with bold confidence, using faith-filled words just like Jesus did.

May 30 – The Lord Is Faithful

But the Lord is faithful, who shall stablish you, and keep you from evil. 2 Thessalonians 3:3

Yet the Lord is faithful, and He will strengthen [you] and set you on a firm foundation and guard you from the evil [one]. — Amp

He's a brother and companion in faith. God's man in spreading the Message, preaching Christ. — Message

But the Lord is to be relied on...give you strength and protect you from the evil one. — Gspd

...but the Lord keeps faith with us. — Knox

...He will give you strength, and guard you from Evil. — TCNT

...fortify you and guard you from the evil one. — NEB

I decree the Lord is faithful towards me. I decree God is strengthening me; guarding me from Satan, the evil one; and He is setting me on a firm foundation.

May 31 – Jesus Is Trustworthy

Blessed is the man that maketh the Lord his trust... Psalm 40:4a

Blessed (happy, fortunate, to be envied) is the man who makes the Lord his refuge and trust... — Amp

Blessed are you who give yourselves over to God... — Message

How happy is the man who hath made Yahweh his confidence... — Rhm

Happy the man who has made Jehovah his trust... — ABPS

O the blessedness of the man who maketh Jehovah his trust... — DeW

I decree I am blessed. I decree I am happy, fortunate, and to be envied by all men because I put my trust in Jesus Christ. I decree He is my Refuge and I do not fear anything.

JUNE

Be there for me,
my God, for I keep
trusting in You.
Don't allow
my foes
to gloat over me
or the shame
of defeat to
overtake me.
Could anyone be
disgraced
when He has
entwined His
heart with yours?
But my foes
will all be
defeated and
ashamed when
they harm the
innocent.
Psalm 25:2-3

June 1 – Rejoicing In The Harvest

He that goeth forth and weepeth, bearing precious seed, shall doubtless come again with rejoicing, bringing his sheaves with him. Psalm 126:6

He who goes forth bearing seed and weeps [at needing his precious supply of grain for sowing], shall doubtless come again with rejoicing, bringing his sheaves with him. — Amp

So those who went off with heavy hearts will come home laughing, with armloads of blessing. — Message

They went step by step and wept sowing their seed; but let them come tripping with joy, carrying their sheaves. — Sept

They went away, went away weeping, carrying the seed; they come back, come back singing, carrying their sheaves. — Jerus

Although they go forth weeping, carrying the seed to be sown, they shall come back rejoicing, carrying their sheaves. — NAB

I decree I may be sowing my seeds in tears; however, I decree I am rejoicing and singing as I am believing that I am receiving a great, abundant harvest!

June 2 – Sacrifices Of Praise

By Him therefore let us offer the sacrifice of praise to God continually, that is, the fruit of our lips giving thanks to His name. Hebrews 13: 15

Through Him, therefore, let us constantly and at all times offer up to God a sacrifice of praise, which is the fruit of lips that thankfully acknowledge and confess and glorify His name. — Amp

God takes particular pleasure in acts of worship - a different kind of "sacrifice" - that take place in kitchen and workplace and on the streets. — Message

So then, through Christ...always offer God the sacrifice of praise...the speech of lips that glorify the name of God. — Wms

...continually lay on the altar a sacrifice of praise to God... — Wey

...at all times present a praise offering to God which is the fruit of lips that make confession in His name. — Ber

I decree I am continuously offering up the sacrifices of praise to God. I decree my lips are continually acknowledging and glorifying His name.

June 3 – Learning To Profit

Thus saith the Lord, thy Redeemer, the Holy One of Israel; I am the Lord thy God which teacheth thee to profit, which leadeth thee by the way that thou should go. Isaiah 48:17

Thus says the Lord, your Redeemer, the Holy One of Israel; I am the Lord your God, who teaches you to profit. Who leads you in the way that you should go. — Amp

And now, the Master, God, sends Me and His Spirit with this Message from God, your Redeemer, The Holy of Israel: 'I am God, your God who teaches you how to live right and well. I show you what to do, where to go.' — Message

This is the word of the Eternal your deliver, the Majestic One of Israel; I am the Eternal God, training you for your good, leading you by the right way. — Mof

I decree Jesus is my Lord and Redeemer. I decree He is teaching me to profit in everything I do. I decree He is leading me in the way I should go, and He is training me how to live right and live well.

June 4 – Continual Deliverance

Many are the afflictions of the righteous: but the Lord delivereth him out of them all. Psalm 34:19

Many evils confront the [consistently] righteous, but the Lord delivers him out of them all. — Amp

Disciples so often get into trouble; still, God is there every time. — Message

Many are the misfortunes of the righteous, but out of them all doth Yahweh rescue him. — Rhm

The good man may have many a mishap, but from them all the Eternal rescues him. — Mof

I decree Father God is my Deliverer. I decree I may be confronted with many misfortunes or troubles in my life but, God delivers me out of all my mishaps. I decree He rescues me from them every time.

June 5 – He's Done Great Things

Then was our mouth filled with laughter, and our tongue with singing: then said they among the heathen, the Lord hath done great things for them. Psalm 126:2

Then were our mouths filled with laughter, and our tongues with singing. Then they said among the nations, The Lord has done great things for them. — Amp

We laughed, we sang, we couldn't believe our good fortune. We were the talk of the nations - "God was wonderful to them!" — Message

Then was our mouth filled with laughter and our tongue with a shout of triumph... — Rhm

In every mouth was laughter, joy was on every tongue... — Knox

Our mouths will be full of laughter, and our tongues with exclamations of joy... — Har

I decree the Lord is doing great things for me! I decree I am rejoicing and singing of His goodness to me! I decree my mouth is full of laughter, and my tongue is triumphantly shouting a victory song. I decree I am full of joy!

June 6 – Faith Words

But what saith it? The word is nigh thee, even in thy mouth, and in thy heart: that is, the word of faith, which we preach. Romans 10:8

The Word (God's message in Christ) is near you, on your lips and in your heart; that is, the Word (the message, the basis and object) of faith which we preach. — Amp

The word that saves is right here, as near as the tongue in your mouth, as close as the heart in your chest. It's the word of faith that welcomes God to go to work and set things right for us. This is the core of our preaching. — Message

God's message is close to you, on your lips and in your mind...the message about faith that we preach. — Gspd

...is already within easy reach of each of us; in fact, it is as near as our own ears, and mouths. — Tay

...which means The Message of Faith, which we proclaim. — TCNT

I decree God's Word is continually in my heart and on my lips. I decree it is the foundation of my faith. I decree my faith-filled words cause God to work for me and set things right.

June 7 – Sing A New Victory Song

O sing unto the Lord a new song; for He hath done marvellous things: His right hand, and His holy arm hath gotten Him the victory.
Psalm 98:1

O Sing to the Lord a new song, for He has done marvelous things; His right hand and His holy arm have wrought salvation for Him. — Amp

Sing to God a brand-new song. He's made a world of wonders! He rolled up His sleeves, He set things right. — Message

Sing ye to Jehovah a new song, for wonders He hath done... — YLT

...His right hand and His holy arm have brought Him victory... — AAT

...His great power and supreme strength have achieved victory for Him... — Har

...for He has won a mighty victory by His power and holiness... — Tay

I decree I am singing a new song in my heart to God. I decree He has done marvelous things for me. I decree He has turned my life around with His great power and supreme strength. I decree He has given me the victory.

June 8 – My Heart's Desires

Grant thee according to Thine own heart, and fulfill all Thy counsel. Psalm 20:4

May He grant you according to your heart's desire and fulfill all your plans. — Amp

Give you what your heart desires, accomplish your plans. — Message

May He grant you your heart's desire, and fulfill all your plans! — RSV

May He grant you your heart's desire, and crown all your plans with success. — Jerus

I decree God is giving me the desires of my heart. I decree He is accomplishing all of my plans. I decree I am successful, and I cannot fail.

June 9 – Created For Good Works

For we are His workmanship, created in Christ Jesus unto good works, which God hath before ordained that we should walk in them. Ephesians 2:10

For we are God's [own] handiwork (His workmanship) recreated in Christ Jesus, [born anew] that we may do those good works which God predestined (planned beforehand) for us [taking paths which He prepared ahead of time], that we should walk in them [living the good life which He prearranged and made ready for us to live]. — Amp

He creates each of us by Christ Jesus to join Him in the work He does, the good work He has gotten ready for us to do, work we had better be doing. — Message

God has created us in Christ Jesus, pledged to such good actions as He has prepared beforehand, to be the employment of our lives. — Knox

I decree I am God's handiwork, His own workmanship. I decree He designed me and recreated me in Christ Jesus to do the good works He planned and predestined for me to walk in. I decree I am living the good life He has prepared for me.

June 10 – Walk In Love

And walk in love, as Christ also hath loved us, and hath given Himself for us an offering and a sacrifice to God for a sweet smelling savior. Ephesians 5:2

And walk in love, [esteeming and delighting in one another] as Christ loved us and gave Himself up for us, a slain offering and sacrifice to God [for you, so that it became] a sweet fragrance. — Amp

Mostly what God does is love you. Keep company with Him and learn a life of love. Observe how Christ loved us. His love was not cautious but extravagant. He didn't love in order to get something from us but to give everything of Himself to us. Love like that. — Message

And give Himself to God as a sacrifice to take away your sins. And God was pleased, for Christ's love for you was like a sweet perfume to Him. — Tay

I decree I am loving others. I decree I am esteeming them and delighting in them just like Jesus loved me and gave His life for me. I decree I am not cautious with my love. I decree I love extravagantly, not thinking of myself, but giving to others.

June 11 – Inherit The Promises

That ye be not slothful, but followers of them who through faith and patience inherit the promises. Hebrews 6:12

In order that you may not grow disinterested and become [spiritual] sluggards, but imitators, behaving as do those who through faith (by their leaning of the entire personality on God in Christ in absolute trust and confidence in His power, wisdom, and goodness) and by practice of patient endurance and waiting are [now] inheriting the promises. — Amp

Don't drag your feet. Be like those who stay the course with committed faith and then get everything promised to them. — Message

That ye be not sluggish but imitators of them who through faith and patience. — ASV

...so that you may not become half-hearted...are heirs to the promises. — Wey

I decree I am not growing disinterested or becoming a sluggard who is spiritually lazy. I decree I am putting my faith, confidence, and trust in the power, wisdom, and goodness of Jesus. I decree I am practicing patient endurance, so I inherit all of God's promises.

June 12 – Blessed While I Sleep

It is vain for you to rise up early, to sit up late, to eat the bread of sorrows: for so He giveth His beloved sleep. Psalm 127:2

It is vain for you to rise up early, to take rest late, to eat the bread of [anxious] toil – for He gives [blessings] to His beloved in sleep. — Amp

It's useless to rise early and go to bed late, and work your worried fingers to the bone. — Message

Vain is it to rise early for your work, and keep at work so late, gaining your bread with anxious toil! — Mof

It is senseless for you to work so hard from early morning until late at night, fearing you will starve to death. — Tay

...since He provides for His beloved as they sleep. — Jerus

...for God wants His loved ones to get their proper rest. — Tay

I decree I am I prospering while I sleep. I decree I am working peacefully and confidently, knowing Jesus blesses me in everything I do. I decree I am increasing as I rest.

June 13 — Prosperous And Healthy

Beloved, I wish above all things that thou mayest prosper and be in health, even as thy soul prospereth. 3 John 2

Beloved, I pray that you may prosper in every way and [that your body] may keep well, even as [I know] your soul keeps well and prospers. — Amp

We're the best of friends, and I pray for good fortune in everything you do, and for your good health - that your everyday affairs prosper, as well as your soul! — Message

Dear friend, I pray that all may be well with you and that you may have good health - I know that all is well with your soul. — TCNT

Dearly loved one, I pray that you may in all respects prosper and keep well... — Wey

...as indeed your soul is keeping well. — Mof

I decree My soul is well and prospering daily. I decree I am increasing and prospering in every way, and I am enjoying good health.

June 14 – Come Out Of Distresses

Then they cry unto the Lord in their trouble, and He bringeth them out of their distresses.
Psalm 107:28

Then they cry to the Lord in their trouble, and He brings them out of their distresses. — Amp

Then you called out to God in your desperate condition; He got you out in the nick of time. — Message

Then make they outcry to Yahweh in their peril, And out of their distresses He bringeth them forth. — Rhm

I decree I am calling to Father God in my desperate condition. I decree I am confident He hears me and I know He is delivering me out of all my troubles and distresses in the nick of time.

June 15 – Full Of Belief

Let us draw near with a true heart in full assurance of faith, having our hearts sprinkled from an evil conscience, and our bodies washed with pure water. Hebrews 10:22

Let us all come forward and draw near with true (honest and sincere) hearts in unqualified assurance and absolute conviction engendered by faith (by that leaning of the entire human personality on God in absolute trust and confidence in His power, wisdom, and goodness), having our hearts sprinkled and purified from a guilty (evil) conscience and our bodies cleansed with pure water. — Amp

So let's do it - full of belief, confident that we're presentable inside and out. — Message

...purified by the sprinkled Blood from all consciousness of wrong. — TCNT

...sprinkled clean from consciences oppressed with sin. — Wey

I decree I am drawing near to God with a true, honest, and sincere heart. I decree I am coming boldly and confidently into the presence of God by faith, knowing my heart is purified from a guilty conscience. I decree I have been cleansed by the Blood of Jesus and my body is cleansed with pure water.

June 16 – Nothing To Fear

Be not afraid of sudden fear, neither of the desolation of the wicked when it cometh. Proverbs 3:25

Be not afraid of sudden terror and panic, nor of the stormy blast or the storm and ruin of the wicked when it comes [for you will be guiltless]. — Amp

No need to panic over alarms or surprises, or predictions that doomsday's just around the corner. — Message

Be not thou afraid of sudden dread, nor of the desolation of the lawless; when it cometh. — Rhm

Do not be afraid of sudden panic, or of the ruin of the wicked, when it comes. — RSV

You will fear no sudden terror, nor the storm that falls on the wicked. — AAT

I decree I am not afraid, in terror or in sudden panic when unexpected things happen. I decree the peace of God rules in my heart and mind. I decree I am not in fear, nor do I panic in my mind when I hear predictions of ruin or unexpected storms coming.

June 17 – Entrusted To God

And now, brethren, I commend you to God, and to the word of His grace, which is able to build you up, and to give you an inheritance among all them which are sanctified. Acts 20:32

...And now [brethren], I commit you to God [I deposit you in His charge, entrusting you to His protection and care]. And I commend you to the Word of His grace [to the commands and counsels and promises of His unmerited favor]. It is able to build you up and give you [your rightful] inheritance among all God's set-apart ones (those consecrated, purified, and transformed of soul). — Amp

"Now I'm turning you over to God, our marvelous God whose gracious Word can make you into what He wants you to be and give you everything you could possibly need in this community of holy friends." — Message

...I entrust you to God... — Mof

I decree I am entrusted to God's care. I decree He is protecting and caring for me. I decree I am renewing my mind with His Word so He can make me into the person He wants me to be. I decree His grace gives me the commands, counsels, and promises of His unmerited favor. I decree He gives me everything I possibly need.

June 18 – God Is Faithful

Faithful is He that calleth you, who also will do it. 1 Thessalonians 5:24

Faithful is He Who is calling you [to Himself] and utterly trustworthy, and He will also do it [fulfill His call by hallowing and keeping you]. — Amp

The One who called you is completely dependable. If He said it, He'll do it! — Message

He who calls you will not fail you, He will complete His work. — TCNT

...He will fulfill my prayer. — Con

I decree I am putting my faith in God. I decree He is faithful, trustworthy, and dependable. I decree He will never fail me. I decree He will always keep me and do what He says He will do. I decree He is completing what He started in me.

June 19 – Faith Makes You Whole

And Jesus said unto him, Go thy way; they faith hath made thee whole. And immediately he received his sight, and followed Jesus in the way. Mark 10:52

And Jesus said to him, Go your way; your faith has healed you. And at once he received his sight and accompanied Jesus on the road. — Amp

"On your way," said Jesus. "Your faith has saved and healed you." In that very instant he recovered his sight and followed Jesus down the road. — Message

...go your way your faith has made you well... — RSV

...go; your faith has cured you... — NEB

...Go! Your faith has restored you... — Ber

...instantly he regained his sight... — Wey

...and all at once he could see again... — Wms

I decree Jesus is my Healer. I decree I am full of faith, and I have enough faith to receive my healing. I decree I believe I am receiving my healing right now. I decree my faith in God's promises works every time.

June 20 – The Love Of God

And hope maketh not ashamed; because the love of God is shed abroad in our hearts by the Holy Ghost which is given unto us. Romans 5:5

Such hope never disappoints or deludes or shames us, for God's love has been poured out in our hearts through the Holy Spirit Who has been given to us. — Amp

In alert expectancy such as this, we're never left feeling shortchanged. Quite the contrary - we can't round up enough containers to hold everything God generously pours into our lives through the Holy Spirit. — Message

...and that hope never disappoints... — TCNT

...since God's love floods our hearts through the Holy Spirit which has been given to us. — Mof

I decree I am putting my hope in Jesus, so I am never disappointed or left feeling short-changed by Him. I decree God's love, through the Holy Spirit, is being poured out into my heart. I decree I am receiving everything God generously pours into my life.

June 21 – He Healed Them

And the people, when they knew it, followed Him: and He received them, and spake unto them of the kingdom of God, and healed them that had need of healing. Luke 9:11

But when the crowds learned of it [they] followed Him; and He welcomed them and talked to them about the kingdom of God, and healed those who needed restoration to health. — Amp

But the crowds got wind of it and followed. Jesus graciously welcomed them and talked to them about the kingdom of God. Those who needed healing, He healed. — Message

But the people recognized Him and followed Him in the crowds... — TCNT

...and He welcomed them... — RSV

...He received them kindly... — Mon

I decree I am following Jesus. I decree He graciously welcomes me into His family with His love. I decree He talks to me about His Kingdom, and He is completely restoring me to perfect health.

June 22 – Life And Godliness

According as His divine power hath given unto us all things that pertain to life and godliness, through the knowledge of Him that hath called us to glory and virtue. 2 Peter 1:3

For His divine power has bestowed upon us all things that [are requisite and suited] to life and godliness, through the [full, personal] knowledge of Him Who called us by and to His own glory and excellence (virtue). — Amp

Everything that goes into a life of pleasing God has been miraculously given to us by getting to know, personally and intimately, the One who invited us to God. The best invitation you ever received! — Message

For His divine power has given us everything that is needful for a life of piety as we advance in the knowledge of Him who called us by a glorious manifestation of His goodness. — TCNT

I decree God's miraculous, Divine power is giving me everything I need to live a Godly life. I decree I am getting to know God personally and intimately which is the best invitation I have ever received.

June 23 – God's My Shield

Every word of God is pure: He is a shield unto them that put their trust in Him. Proverbs 30:5

Every word of God is tried and purified; He is a shield to those who trust and take refuge in Him. — Amp

The believer replied, "Every promise of God proves true; He protects everyone who runs to Him for help." — Message

Every word of God is tested; He is a shield to those who take refuge in Him. — NASB

I decree I am putting my trust in God's Word. I decree every promise of God is tested and proven to be true. I decree God is my Shield and Refuge and I run to Him for help, I decree He protects me from all the enemy's attacks.

June 24 – Good Advice

I [the Lord] will instruct you and teach you in the way you should go; I will counsel you with My eye upon you. Psalm 32:8

I [the Lord] will instruct you and teach you in the way you should go; I will counsel you with My eye upon you. — Amp

Let me give you some good advice; I'm looking you in the eye and giving it to you straight. — Message

I will instruct you and teach you in the way which you should go; I will counsel you with My eye upon you. – NASB

I decree the Lord is instructing and teaching me in the way I should go. I decree He is leading me, guiding me, and counseling me. I decree His watchful eyes are always upon of me.

June 25 – God's Spirit Helps Us

Likewise the Spirit also helpeth our infirmities: for we know not what we should pray for as we ought: but the Spirit itself maketh intercession for us with groanings which cannot be uttered. Romans 8:26

So too the [Holy] Spirit comes to our aid and bears us up in our weakness; for we do not know what prayer to offer nor how to offer it worthily as we ought, but the Spirit Himself goes to meet our supplication and pleads in our behalf with unspeakable yearnings and groanings to keep for utterance. — Amp

Meanwhile, the moment we get tired in the waiting, God's Spirit is right alongside helping us along. If we don't know how or what to pray, it doesn't matter. He does our praying in and for us, making prayer out of our wordless sighs, our aching groans. — Message

The Spirit of God not only maintains this hope within us, but helps us in our present limitations... — Phi

I decree I am waiting patiently with Holy Spirit helping me in my weaknesses. I decree He intercedes for me with unspeakable yearnings and groaning when I don't know how or what to pray for myself.

June 26 – Completely Sanctified

And the very God of peace sanctify you wholly; and I pray God your whole spirit and soul and body be preserved blameless unto the coming of our Lord Jesus Christ. 1 Thessalonians 5:23

And may the God of peace Himself sanctify you through and through [separate you from profane things, make you pure and wholly consecrated to God]; and may your spirit and soul and body be preserved sound and complete [and found] blameless at the coming of our Lord Jesus Christ (the Messiah). — Amp

May God Himself, the God who makes everything holy and whole, make you holy and whole, put you together - spirit, soul, and body - and keep you fit for the coming of our Master, Jesus Christ. — Message

...and the God of peace Himself, he be preserved entire, without blame... — ASV

May the God of peace consecrate you through and through... — Mof

I decree I am sanctified and set apart for God. I decree I am holy, whole, completely put together - spirit, soul, body - by God Himself. I decree He makes me complete for the coming of my Lord and Master, Jesus Christ.

June 27 – Rejoice In Goodness

That I may see the good of Thy chosen, that I may rejoice in the gladness of Thy nation, that I may glory with thine inheritance. Psalm 106:5

That I may see and share the welfare of Your chosen ones, that I may rejoice in the gladness of Your nation, that I may glory with Your heritage. — Amp

I want to see your chosen succeed, celebrate with your celebrating nation, join the Hallelujahs of your pride and joy! — Message

That I may look upon the welfare of Thy chosen ones, that I may rejoice in the joy of Thy nation, that I may glory with Thine inheritance. — Rhm

That I may see the prosperity of Thy chosen, rejoice in Thy nation's joy and exult with Thy own people. — NEB

I decree I am celebrating with God in that He has chosen me to prosper and succeed. I decree I am rejoicing and praising God with gladness that this is my inheritance.

June 28 – Kingdom Of God

For the kingdom of God is not meat and drink; but righteousness, and peace, and joy in the Holy Ghost. Romans 14:17

[After all] the kingdom of God is not a matter of [getting the] food and drink [one likes], but instead it is righteousness (that state which makes a person acceptable to God) and [heart] peace and joy in the Holy Spirit. — Amp

God's kingdom isn't a matter of what you put in your stomach, for goodness' sake. It's what God does with your life as He sets it right, puts it together, and completes it with joy. — Message

...but the righteousness and peace and gladness through the presence of the Holy Spirit. — TCNT

...it means rightness of heart, finding our peace and our joy in the Holy Spirit. — Knox

I decree I am operating in the Kingdom of God. I decree I am full of peace, righteousness, and joy in the presence of Holy Spirit. I decree God is setting my life right as He puts it all together and completes it with joy.

June 29 – Free From Debt

The rich ruleth over the poor, and the borrow-
er is servant to the lender. Proverbs 22:7

The rich rule over the poor, and the borrower is servant
to the lender. — Amp

The poor are always ruled over by the rich, so don't bor-
row and put yourself under their power. — Message

The rich rules over the poor, and the borrower is the
slave to the lender. — RSV

The man of wealth has rule over the poor, and he who
gets into debt is a servant to his creditor. — Bas

Just as the rich rule the poor, so the borrower is servant
to the lender. — Tay

Rich rules poor, debtor must wait on creditor. — Knox

I decree I am delivered from the curse of the Law and
the spirit of poverty, lack, and debt against my life. I
decree I am free from debt, and I am not a slave to the
lender.

June 30 – Send Forth Laborers

Pray ye therefore the Lord of the harvest, that He will send forth labourers into His harvest.
Matthew 9:38

So pray to the Lord of the harvest to force out and thrust laborers into His harvest. — Amp

"What a huge harvest!" He said to His disciples. "How few workers! On your knees and pray for harvest hands!" — Message

Therefore urge the owner of the harvest to bring more laborers to His harvest. — Lam

...the Lord to whom the harvest belongs. — Knox

...thrust forth... — Rhm

...for the harvesting. — Knox

I decree God is the Lord of the harvest. I decree He is sending laborers out into the harvest field to bring in the harvest of souls.

JULY

*Such love
has no
fear,
because
perfect love
expels all fear.
If we are
afraid,
it is for
fear of
punishment,
and this
shows that
we have
not
fully
experienced
His
perfect
love.
I John 4:18*

July 1 – Whole Heart Praises

I will praise Thee, O Lord, with my whole heart; I will shew forth all Thy marvellous works. Psalm 9:1

I will praise You, O Lord, with my whole heart; I will show forth (recount and tell aloud) all Your marvelous works and wonderful deeds! — Amp

I'm thanking you, God, from a full heart, I'm writing the book on your wonders. — Message

I will praise Yahweh with all my heart, I will recount all Thy wonderful doings. — Rhm

I thank you, Yahweh, with all my heart; I recite your marvels one by one. — Jerus

I decree I am praising the Lord, with my whole heart. I decree I will tell everyone again and again of all the wonderfully marvelous things He has done for me.

July 2 – Steadfast And Unmovable

Therefore, My beloved, brethren, be ye stead-fast, unmovable, always abounding in the work of the Lord, forasmuch as ye know that your labour is not in vain in the Lord. 1 Corinthians 15:58

Therefore, My beloved brethren, be firm (steadfast), immovable, always abounding in the work of the Lord [always being superior, excelling, doing more than enough in the service of the Lord], knowing and being continually aware that your labor in the Lord is not futile [it is never wasted or to no purpose]. — Amp

And don't hold back. Throw yourselves into the work of the Master, confident that nothing you do for Him is a waste of time or effort. — Message

Since future victory is sure... — Tay

...be strong in purpose... — Bas

...let nothing move you... — Beck

I decree I am strong in purpose; steadfast, immovable, abounding in the work of the Lord. I decree I am always being superior, excelling, and doing more than enough in the service of the Lord. I decree my work is not futile. I decree it is producing a great harvest.

July 3 – All Things To Enjoy

Charge them that are rich in this world, that they be not highminded, nor trust in uncertain riches, but in the living God, who giveth us richly all things to enjoy. 1 Timothy 6:17

As for the rich in this world, charge them not to be proud and arrogant and contemptuous of others, nor to set their hopes on uncertain riches, but on God, Who richly and ceaselessly provides us with everything for [our] enjoyment. — Amp

Tell those rich in this world 's wealth to quit being so full of themselves and so obsessed with money, which is here today and gone tomorrow. Tell them to go after God, who piles on all the riches we could ever manage - to do good, to be rich in helping others, to be extravagantly generous. — Message

...who richly provides us with all the joys of life. — Mof

...who generously gives us everything. — Phi

I decree I do not put my trust in money. I decree I am going after God and putting my trust in Him. I decree He piles on all the riches I could ever manage. I decree I am doing good, helping others, and I am extravagantly generous.

July 4 – Abundant Life

The thief cometh not, but for to steal, and to kill, and to destroy: I am come that they might have life, and that they might have it more abundantly. John 10:10

The thief comes only in order to steal and kill and destroy. I came that they may have and enjoy life, and have it in abundance (to the full, till it overflows). — Amp

A thief is only there to steal and kill and destroy. I came so they can have real and eternal life, more and better life than they ever dreamed of. — Message

The thief comes only to take the sheep and to put them to death; he comes for their destruction. — Bas

...and have it abundantly. — RSV

...and have it overflowing in them. — Beck

My purpose is to give eternal life - abundantly! — Tay

I decree Satan is defeated in my life. I decree Jesus is giving me the abundant life with overflow blessings. I decree I have eternal life and my earthly life is better than I ever dreamed possible.

July 5 – Renew Your Mind

**And be renewed in the spirit of your mind.
Ephesians 4:23**

And be constantly renewed in the spirit of your mind
[having a fresh mental and spiritual attitude]. — Amp

A life renewed from the inside and working itself into
your conduct as God accurately reproduces His character in you. — Message

You must adopt a new attitude of mind. — Gspd

And, with yourselves mentally and spiritually remade.
— Phi

That the very spirit of your minds must be constantly
renewed. — TCNT

*I decree I am renewing my mind with the Word of God
so I have a fresh mental and spiritual attitude. I decree
I am being renewed from the inside out with God's
Word which helps my character become His character.*

July 6 – Keep My Words

Jesus answered and said unto him, If a man love Me, he will keep My words: and My Father will love him, and we will come unto him, and make our abode with him. John 14:23

Jesus answered, If a person [really] loves Me, he will keep My word [obey My teaching]; and My Father will love him, and We will come to him and make Our home (abode, special dwelling place) with him. — Amp

"Because a loveless world, "said Jesus, "is a sightless world. If anyone loves Me, he will carefully keep My word and My Father will love him - we'll move right into the neighborhood! — Message

If anyone loves Me, he will keep My word... — ABUV

...anyone who loves Me will heed what I say...and make our dwelling with him. — NEB

I decree I am loving Jesus, and I am obeying His teachings. I decree Father God loves me and He, Jesus, and Holy Spirit are living in me.

July 7 – Uncontainable Blessings

Bring ye all the tithes into the storehouse, that there may be meat in mine house, and prove me now herewith, saith the Lord of hosts, if I will not open you the windows of heaven, and pour you out a blessing, that there shall not be room enough to receive it. Malachi 3:10

Bring all the tithes (the whole tenth of your income) into the storehouse, that there may be food in My house, and prove Me now by it, says the Lord of hosts, if I will not open the windows of heaven for you and pour you out a blessing, that there shall not be room enough to receive it. — Amp

Bring your full tithe to the Temple treasury so there will be ample provisions in My Temple. Test Me in this and see if I don't open up heaven itself to you and pour out blessings beyond your wildest dreams. — Message

...and then see if I don't open the floodgates of heaven for you and pour out blessing for you in abundance. — Jerus

I decree I am a tither. I decree I am bringing all my tithe into the storehouse and God is opening the floodgates of heaven pouring out blessings on me that are beyond my wildest dreams.

July 8 – Love Covers Sin

And above all things have fervent charity among yourselves: for charity shall cover the multitude of sins. 1 Peter 4:8

Above all things have intense and unfailing love for one another, for love covers a multitude of sins [forgives and disregards the offense of others]. — Amp

Most of all, love each other as if your life depended on it. Love makes up for practically anything. — Message

Above all things being fervent in your love among yourselves... — ASV

...keep your love for one another strong... — Gspd

...for Love throws a veil over countless sins. — TCNT

...love hides a host of sins. — Mof

...love cancels innumerable sins. — NEB

I decree I am loving others with the Godkind of love. I decree I am walking in the love of God which enables me to cover a multitude of sins and forgive others of any offenses they bring my way.

July 9 – His Healing Word

He sent His word, and healed them and delivered them from their destructions. Psalm 107:20

He sends forth His word and heals them and rescues them from the pit and destruction. — Amp

He spoke the word that healed you, that pulled you back from the brink of death. — Message

He sendeth His word, and healeth them, and delivereth them from their dangers. — DeW

He sent forth His word to heal them and to snatch them from destruction. — NAB

He sent out His word to heal them and to save their lives from the grave. — Ber

I decree I am speaking God's Word and sending it out into the atmosphere. I decree His Word is bringing healing to my mind and body, and is delivering me from destruction.

July 10 – The Lord Hears

This poor man cried, and the Lord heard him, and saved him out of all his troubles. Psalm 34:6

This poor man cried, and the Lord heard him, and saved him out of all his troubles. — Amp

When I was desperate, I called out, and God got me out of a tight spot. — Message

The sufferer called, and Jehovah heard... — ABPS

This oppressed one cried, and Yahweh heard, and out of all his distresses saved him. — Rhm

Here is a poor man whose cry the Eternal heard, and helped him out of all his troubles. — Mof

Friendless folk may still call upon the Lord and gain his ear, and be rescued from all their afflictions. — Knox

I decree I am calling out to the Lord, and He is hearing me. I decree He is delivering me out of all my troubles, distresses, and afflictions.

July 11 – Shout For Joy

Because thou hast been my help, therefore in the shadow of Thy wings will I rejoice. Psalm 63:7

For You have been my help, and in the shadow of Your wings will I rejoice. — Amp

It's time to shout praises! If I'm sleepless at midnight, I spend the hours in grateful reflection. — Message

For thou hast become a help unto me, and in the shadow of Thy wings will I shout for joy. — Rhm

For since Thou hast become my helper, overshadowed by Thy wings, I sing for joy. — DeW

For You have been of assistance to me, and under Your mighty protection I shout for joy. — Har

That you are my help, and in the shadow of your wings I shout for joy. — NAB

I decree I am rejoicing and shouting praises to Father God. I decree He is my help in times of need. I decree I am hiding myself under the shadow of His mighty protection and I shout for joy.

July 12 – Whom Shall I Fear

The Lord is my Light and my Salvation; whom shall I fear? The Lord is the strength of my life; of whom shall I be afraid? Psalm 27:1

The Lord is my Light and my Salvation - whom shall I fear or dread? The Lord is the Refuge and Stronghold of my life - of whom shall I be afraid? — Amp

Light, space, zest - that's God! So with Him on my side I'm fearless, afraid of no one and nothing. — Message

Yahweh is the refuge of my life, of whom shall I be in dread... — Rhm

Jehovah is the stronghold of my life; of whom shall I be in dread... — ABPS

The Lord is the defender of my life, of whom shall I be afraid... — Sept

Yahweh is the fortress of my life, of whom should I be afraid... — Jerus

I decree I am trusting in God to be my Refuge. I decree He is on my side, and I am fearless. I decree I am afraid of no one and nothing. I decree I do not have anything to dread.

July 13 – Always Triumphant

Now thanks be unto God, which always causeth us to triumph in Christ, and maketh manifest the savour of His knowledge by us in every place. 2 Corinthians 2:14

But thanks be to God, Who in Christ always leads us in triumph [as trophies of Christ's victory] and through us spreads *and* makes evident the fragrance of the knowledge of God everywhere. — Amp

In the Messiah, in Christ, God leads us from place to place in one perpetual victory parade. Through us, He brings knowledge of Christ. Everywhere we go, people breathe in the exquisite fragrance. — Message

...who, through our union with Christ, leads us in one continual triumph. — TCNT

Wherever I go, thank God, He makes my life a constant pageant of triumph in Christ... — Mof

I decree I am thanking God because I am one with Christ. I decree I am triumphant, and He leads me from place to place in one perpetual victory parade. I decree everywhere I go I spread the exquisite fragrance of the knowledge of God.

July 14 – Faith To Enter In

Seeing therefore it remaineth that some must enter therein, and they to whom it was first preached entered not in because of unbelief. Hebrews 4:6

Seeing then that the promise remains over [from past times] for some to enter that rest, and that those who formerly were given the good news about it and the opportunity, failed to appropriate it and did not enter because of disobedience. — Amp

Those earlier ones never did get to the place of rest because they were disobedient. God keeps renewing the promise and setting the date as today, just as He did in David's psalm, centuries later than the original invitation: Today, please listen, don't turn a deaf ear. — Message

Since, then, there is still a promise that some shall enter upon this rest... — TCNT

I decree I am entering into God's rest because I believe His promises are for me, today. I decree I am hearing His Word, obeying His instructions, and entering into His peace.

July 15 – Sing Praises

Praise the Lord; for the Lord is good: sing praises unto His name; for it is pleasant. Psalm 135:3

Praise the Lord! For the Lord is good; sing praises to His name, for He is gracious and lovely! — Amp

Shout "Hallelujah!" because God's so good, sing anthems to His beautiful name. — Message

Praise ye Yah, for good is Yahweh. Sing praises to His Name. For it is full of delight. — Rhm

Hallelujah; for Jehovah is good; Sing praises unto His Name, for it is delightful. — Sprl

Praise the Lord, for that is good. Honour His name with psalms, for that is pleasant. — NEB

May God be praised. The Lord is good; sing praise to His name, for to do so is appropriate. — Har

I decree I am praising the Lord because He is good all the time. I decree I am singing His praises because I am honoring His name with all my heart. I decree I am worshipping Him with all my heart. Hallelujah!

July 16 – Free Indeed

If the Son therefore shall make you free, ye shall be free indeed. John 8:36

So if the Son liberates you [makes you free men], then you are really and unquestionably free. — Amp

So if the Son sets you free, you are free through and through. — Message

So if the Son makes you free... — RSV

...you will be truly free. — Bas

So if the Son liberates you, then you are unquestionably free. — Ber

I decree the Lord has set me free. I decree He is liberating me from the enemy's grip and is setting me gloriously and totally free. I decree I am, indeed, unquestionably free.

July 17 – The Conqueror's Reward

He that hath an ear, let him hear what the Spirit saith unto the churches; to him that overcometh will I give to eat of the hidden manna, and will give him a white stone, and in the stone a new name written, which no man knoweth saving he that receiveth it. Revelation 2:17

...to him who overcomes (conquers), I will give to eat of the manna that is hidden, and I will give him a white stone with a new name engraved on the stone, which no one knows or understands except he who receives it. — Amp

Are your ears awake? Listen. Listen to the Wind Words, the Spirit blowing through the churches. I'll give the sacred manna to every conqueror; I'll also give a clear, smooth stone inscribed with your new name, your secret new name. — Message

I decree I am a more than a conqueror through Christ Jesus. I decree I am hearing the wind of Holy Spirit blow through me as I feast on God's Word. I decree my new name is written on a smooth stone, and I understand it.

July 18 – Live Free

As free, and not using your liberty for a cloke of maliciousness, but as the servants of God. 1 Peter 2:16

[Live] as free people, [yet] without employing your freedom as a pretext for wickedness; but [live at all times] as servants of God. — Amp

Exercise your freedom by serving God, not by breaking the rules. — Message

Be free men, and yet do not make your freedom a screen for base conduct. — Wey

Live like free men, only never make your freedom a pretext for misconduct. — Mof

Live like free men, only do not make your freedom an excuse for doing wrong, but, be the slaves of God. — Gspd

Act as free men, but do not use your freedom as a cloak to cover up some wickedness. — Nor

I decree I am living a life of freedom. I decree I am making wise choices and I am not breaking the rules. I decree I am an example for others to see God's power and goodness in the earth.

July 19 – From Glory To Glory

But we all, with open face beholding as in a glass the glory of the Lord, are changed into the same image from glory to glory, even as by the Spirit of the Lord. 2 Corinthians 3:18

And all of us, as with unveiled face, [because we] continued to behold [in the Word of God] as in a mirror the glory of the Lord. Are constantly being transfigured into His very own image in ever-increasing splendor and from one degree of glory to another: [for this comes] from the Lord [Who is] the Spirit. — Amp

Nothing between us and God, our faces shining with the brightness of His face. And so we are transfigured much like the Messiah, our lives gradually becoming brighter and more beautiful as God enters our lives and we become like Him. — Message

...we can be mirrors that brightly reflect the glory of the Lord. — Tay

...even as from a Spirit that is Lord. — Rhm

I decree I am meeting God face to face as I read His Word. I decree He is changing me from glory to glory and transforming me into His very image as I allow Him to enter my life.

July 20 – Strong On Our Behalf

For the eyes of the Lord run to and fro throughout the whole earth to shew Himself strong in the behalf of them whose heart is perfect toward Him. 2 Chronicles 16:9

For the eyes of the Lord run to and fro throughout the whole earth to show Himself strong in behalf of those whose hearts are blameless toward Him. — Amp

God is always on the alert, constantly on the lookout for people who are totally committed to Him. You are foolish to go for human help when you could have had God's help. — Message

The eyes of the Lord range through the whole earth, to bring aid and comfort to those whose hearts are loyal to Him. — NEB

For the eyes of the Lord flash back and forth over the whole earth to display His strength on behalf of those whose heart is full of integrity toward Him. — Ber

I decree God's eyes are stopping on me as He looks throughout the whole earth for someone to show Himself strong on their behalf. I decree He is helping me in everything I do because my heart is full of integrity toward Him.

July 21 – Healed All Sickness

When the even was come, they brought unto Him many that were possessed with devils; and He cast out the spirits with His word, and healed all that were sick. Matthew 8:16

When evening came, they brought to Him many who were under the power of demons, and He drove out the spirits with a word and restored to health all who were sick. — Amp

That evening a lot of demon-afflicted people were brought to Him. He relieved the inwardly tormented. He cured the bodily ill. He fulfilled Isaiah's well-known sermon: He took our illnesses, He carried our diseases. — Message

...many who were under the power of demons... — Wms

...a number of people who had evil spirits... — Bas

...and with a word He drove out the evil spirits... — Nor

...indeed, He healed all who were ill. — Phi

I decree Jesus is healing my body right now and He is restoring my mental health from tormenting anxiety. I decree I am delivered from the power of Satan's afflictions.

July 22 – Heartfelt Prayers

Confess your faults one to another, and pray one for another, that ye may be healed. The effectual fervent prayer of a righteous man availeth much. James 5:16

...The earnest (heartfelt, continued) prayer of a righteous man makes tremendous power available [dynamic in its working]. — Amp

The prayer of a person living right with God is something powerful to be reckoned with. — Message

...powerful is the heartfelt supplication of a righteous man. — Wey

...the prayers of the righteous have a powerful effect. — Mof

...tremendous power is made available through a good man's earnest prayer. — Phi

...the prayer of a righteous man has great power in its effects. — RSV

I decree I am righteous, in right standing with God. I decree my prayers are making great power available to others and I am getting answers to my prayers all the time.

July 23 – Keep Your Tongue

For he that will love life, and see good days, let him refrain his tongue from evil, and his lips that they speak no guile. 1 Peter 3:10

For let him who wants to enjoy life and see good days [good-whether apparent or not] keep his tongue free from evil and his lips from guile (treachery, deceit). — Amp

Whoever wants to embrace life and see the day fill up with good, here's what you do: say nothing evil or hurtful; snub evil and cultivate good; run after peace for all you're worth. — Message

He that would enjoy life and see happy days - let him keep his tongue from evil and his lips from deceitful words. — TCNT

I decree I am embracing and enjoying life to the fullest as I keep my tongue from speaking evil words. I decree I am only speaking faith-filled, life-giving words and am following after peace.

July 24 – Christ Made You Free

Stand fast therefore in the liberty wherewith Christ hath made us free, and be not entangled again with the yoke of bondage. Galatians 5:1

In [this] freedom Christ has made us free [and completely liberated us]; stand fast then, and do not be hampered and held ensnared and submit again to a yoke of slavery [which you have once put off]. — Amp

Christ has set us free to live a free life. So take your stand! Never again let anyone put a harness of slavery on you. — Message

For freedom did Christ set us free; stand fast therefore, and be not entangled again in a yoke of bondage. — ASV

Christ has made us completely free; stand fast then, and do not again be hampered with the yoke of slavery. — Wey

This is the freedom with which Christ has freed us... — Gspd

I decree Christ has already set me gloriously free to live a life full of freedom. I decree I am not going to be hampered or ensnared back into a lifestyle of bondage to a yoke of Satan's slavery to anything in my former life.

July 25 – Possess Prosperity

For the seed shall be prosperous; the vine shall give her fruit, and the ground shall give her increase, and the heavens shall give their dew; and I will cause the remnant of this people to possess all these things. Zechariah 8:12

For there shall the seed produce peace and prosperity; the vine shall yield her fruit and the ground shall give its increase and the heavens shall give their dew; and I will cause the remnant of this people to inherit and possess all these things. — Amp

Sowing and harvesting will resume, Vines will grow grapes, gardens will flourish, dew and rain will make everything green. My core survivors will get everything they need - and more. — Message

For there shall be the seed of peace; the vine shall give its fruit, and the ground shall give its increase. — ASV

I decree I am possessing peace and prosperity. I decree my vines will yield their fruit and the ground will give it's increase as the heavens give their dew. I decree I am receiving everything I need to possess prosperity.

July 26 – A Merry Heart

A merry heart doeth good like a medicine; but a broken spirit drieth the bones. Proverbs 17:22

A happy heart is good medicine and a cheerful mind works healing, but a broken spirit dries up the bones. — Amp

A cheerful disposition is good for your health; gloom and doom leave you bone-tired. — Message

A cheerful heart makes a quick recovery, it is crushed spirits that waste a man's frame. — Knox

A merry heart makes a cheerful countenance, but low spirits sap a man's strength. — NEB

A cheerful heart is a good medicine, but a downcast spirit dries up the bones. — RSV

A joyful heart worketh an excellent cure, but a stricken spirit drieth up the bone. — Rhm

I decree I am choosing to have a cheerful disposition, so my heart is continuously happy. I decree my countenance reflects my happy heart which is medicine and health to my bones.

July 27 – Living By Faith

Now the just shall live by faith: but if any man draw back, My soul shall have no pleasure in him. **Hebrews 10:38**

But the just shall live by faith [My righteous servant shall live by his conviction respecting man's relationship to God and divine things, and holy fervor born of faith and conjoined with it]; and if he draws back and shrinks in fear, My soul has no delight or pleasure in him. — Amp

But anyone who is right with Me thrives on loyal trust; if he cuts and runs, I won't be very happy. — Message

But My righteous one by faith shall live and if he draw back My soul delighteth not in him. — Rhm

Meantime My just man is to live on by his faith... — Mof

But the upright man will be living by his faith... — Bas

I decree I am righteous; in right standing with God. I decree I am living my life by faith, trusting God, and I do not draw back or shrink back in fear. I decree God is taking pleasure in me and He delights over me.

July 28 – Praise His Name

I will worship toward Thy holy temple, and praise Thy name for Thy loving-kindness and for Thy truth; for Thou has magnified Thy word above all Thy name. Psalm 183:2

I will worship toward Your holy temple and praise Your name for Your loving-kindness and for your truth and faithfulness; for You have exalted above all else Your name and Your word and You have magnified Your word above all Your name! — Amp

I kneel in worship facing your holy temple, and say it again: "Thank you! "Thank you for your love, thank you for your faithfulness; most holy is your name, most holy is your Word. — Message

...for you have made great above all things your name and your promise. — NAB

...for your promises are backed by all the honor of your name. — Tay

I decree I am praising God for His loving-kindness, truthfulness, and faithfulness to me. I decree I am magnifying His Word, above His name. I decree I am thanking God for His promises to me that are backed by His name.

July 29 – Saved Through Faith

***For by grace are ye saved through faith; and
that not of yourselves: it is the gift of God.
Ephesians 2:8***

For it is by free grace (God's unmerited favor) that you
are saved (delivered from judgment and made par-
takers of Christ's salvation) through, [your] faith. And
this [salvation] is not of yourselves [of your own doing,
it came not through your own striving], but it is the gift
of God. — Amp

Saving is all His idea, and all His work. All we do is
trust Him enough to let Him do it. It's God's gift from
start to finish! — Message

Yes, it was grace that saved you, with faith for its in-
strument it did not come from yourselves... — Knox

For it is by God's loving-kindness that you have been
saved, through your faith. It is not due to yourselves,
the gift is God's. — TCNT

*I decree I am saved by God's loving-kindness. I decree
it is His grace, His unmerited favor, that has saved me
and delivered me from judgment. Through my faith in
Jesus, I decree I am enjoying God's free gift of salvation to me. I cannot earn my salvation.*

July 30 – Captivate Thoughts

Casting down imaginations, and every high thing that exalteth itself against the knowledge of God, and bringing into captivity every thought to the obedience of Christ. 2 Corinthians 10:5

[Inasmuch as we] refute arguments and theories and reasonings and every proud and lofty thing that sets itself up against the [true] knowledge of God; and we lead every thought and purpose away captive into the obedience of Christ (the Messiah, the Anointed One). — Amp

We use our powerful God-tools for smashing warped philosophies, tearing down barriers erected against the truth of God, fitting every loose thought and emotion and impulse into the structure of life shaped by Christ. — Message

Yes, you can pull down the conceits of men, and every barrier of pride which sets itself up against the true knowledge of God, we make every mind surrender to Christ's service. — Knox

I decree I am pulling down every thought that does not line up with the Word of God and is setting itself against the true knowledge of God. I decree I am making my every thought agree with and obey Christ's thoughts.

July 31 – Acknowledge Him

Trust in the Lord with all thine heart; and lean not unto thine own understanding. In all thy ways acknowledge Him, and He shall direct thy paths. Proverbs 3:5-6

Lean on, trust in, and be confident in the Lord with all your heart and mind and do not rely on your own insight or understanding. In all your ways know, recognize, and acknowledge Him, and He will direct and make straight and plain your paths. — Amp

Trust God from the bottom of your heart; don't try to figure out everything on your own. Listen for God's voice in everything you do, everywhere you go; He's the one who will keep you on track. — Message

Rely with all your heart on the Eternal, and never lean on your own insight; have mind of Him wherever you may go, and He will clear the road for you. — Mof

I decree I am acknowledging God and trusting Him with all my heart. I decree I am listening to Him as He leads me everywhere He wants me to go. I decree I am putting all my confidence in Him, and I am not leaning on my own understanding.

AUGUST

*"Dear
woman,"
Jesus
said
to her,
"your
faith
is
great.
Your
request
is
granted."
And
her
daughter
was
instantly
healed.
Matthew 15:28*

August 1 – He Hears You

And this is the confidence that we have in Him, that, if we ask anything according to His will, He heareth us. 1 John 5:14

And this is the confidence (the assurance, the privilege of boldness) which we have in Him: [we are sure] that if we ask anything (make any request) according to His will (in agreement with His own plan), He listens to and hears us. — Amp

And if we're confident that He's listening, we know that what we've asked for is as good as ours. — Message

And this is the confidence with which we approach Him, that whenever we ask anything that is in accordance with His will, He listens to us. — TCNT

I decree I am confident, and I have boldness to know God hears me when I ask Him anything in accordance with His will and in agreement with His plan for me. I decree He listens to me, and He hears me.

August 2 – Hold Your Confidence

Cast not away therefore your confidence, which hath great recompence of reward. Hebrews 10:35

Do not, therefore, fling away your fearless confidence, for it carries a great and glorious compensation of reward. — Amp

So don't throw it all away now. You were sure of yourselves then, it's still a sure thing! — Message

Now do not drop that confidence of yours, it carries with it a rich hope of reward. — Mof

So you must never give up your confident courage, for it holds a rich reward for you. — Wms

Therefore do not cast from you your confident hope for it will receive a vast reward. — Wey

Cast not away therefore your boldness... — ASV

...for it has a great reward awaiting it. — TCNT

I decree I am holding fast to my confident expectation from the Lord. I decree I am steadfast in believing my confidence carries a great and glorious compensation of reward. I decree my answered prayers are a sure thing!

August 3 – Enter Into Rest

For we which have believed do enter into rest, as He said, as I have sworn in My wrath, if they shall enter into My rest; although the works were finished from the foundations of the world. Hebrews 4:3

For we who have believed (adhered to and trusted in and relied on God) do enter that rest... — Amp

If we believe, though, we'll experience that state of resting. But not if we don't have faith. — Message

We are actually entering into that rest, we who have believed... — Mon

For we who have believed are being admitted to that rest... — Wms

It is only as a result of our faith and trust that we are experiencing that rest ... — Phi

For only we who believe God can enter into His place of rest... — Tay

I decree I am believing in, trusting in, and relying on God. I decree I am putting my faith in His abilities, and I am entering into His rest.

August 4 – Enduring Mercy

Praise ye the Lord. O give thanks unto the Lord; for He is good: for His mercy endureth forever. Psalm 106:1

Praise the Lord! (Hallelujah!) O give thanks to the Lord, for He is good; for His mercy and loving-kindness endure forever! — Amp

Hallelujah! Thank God! And why? Because He's good, because His love lasts. — Message

...for His lovingkindness endureth forever. — ASV

...for His steadfast love endures forever! — RSV

I decree I am praising the Lord and I am giving thanks to Him because He is good. I decree His mercy and loving-kindness endure forever!

August 5 – Real Gain

But what things were gain to me, those I counted loss for Christ. Philippians 3:7

But whatever former things I had that might have been gains to me, I have come to consider as [one combined] loss for Christ's sake. — Amp

Yes, all the things I once thought were so important are gone from my life. — Message

But all the things which I once held to be gains, I have now, for Christ's sake, come to count as loss. — TCNT

But all such assets I have written off because of Christ. — NEB

I decree the former things I had, and once thought were so important to me that I counted as gain, I now count them as loss because Christ Jesus is more important to me.

August 6 – Divine Protection

A thousand may fall at thy side, and ten thousand at thy right hand; but it shall not come nigh thee. Psalm 91:7

A thousand may fall at your side, and ten thousand at your right hand, but it shall not come near you. — Amp

Even though others succumb all around, drop like flies right and left, no harm will even graze you. — Message

Hundreds may fall beside you, thousands at your right hand, but the plague will never reach you. — Mof

Though a thousand fall at your side, ten thousand at your right hand, you yourself will remain unscathed. — Jerus

I decree that I am protected. I decree that thousands and tens of thousands may fall all around me, but no plague or sickness will come near me.

August 7 – Lacking Nothing

The young lions do lack, and suffer hunger: but they that seek the Lord shall not want any good thing. Psalm 34:10

The young lions lack food and suffer hunger, but they who seek (inquire of and require) the Lord [by right of their need and on the authority of His Word], none of them shall lack any beneficial thing. — Amp

Young lions on the prowl get hungry, but God-seekers are full of God. — Message

Unbelievers suffer want and grow hungry, but those who seek the Lord lack no good thing. — NEB

The renegade may be in need, and go hungry; but those who search for the Lord shall not be short of anything good. — Har

The great grow poor and hungry; but those who seek the Lord want for no good thing. — NAB

I decree I am seeking the Lord. I decree I am inquiring of Him and requiring of Him on the authority of His Word. I decree I am lacking no good or beneficial thing. I decree I am full of God. I do not want for anything, nor do I go hungry.

August 8 – Victory Through Jesus

But thanks be to God, which giveth us the victory through our Lord Jesus Christ. 1 Corinthians 15:57

But thanks be to God, Who gives us the victory [making us conquerors] through our Lord Jesus Christ. — Amp

But now in a single victorious stroke of Life, all three - sin, guilt, death - are gone, the gift of our Master, Jesus Christ. Thank God! — Message

But thank God! — Beck

But unto God be thanks... — Rhm

The victory is ours...He makes it ours by our Lord Jesus Christ. — Mof

I decree I am giving God thanks because He is always giving me the victory over sin, guilt, and death. I decree He is making me a conqueror through my Lord Jesus Christ.

August 9 – Labor To Enter Rest

Let us labour therefore to enter into that rest, lest any man fall after the same example of unbelief. Hebrews 4:11

Let us therefore be zealous and exert ourselves and strive diligently to enter that rest [of God to know and experience it for ourselves], that no one may fall or perish by the same kind of unbelief and disobedience [into which those in the wilderness fell]. — Amp

The promise of "arrival" and "rest" is still there for God's people. God Himself is at rest. And at the end of the journey, we will surely rest with God. So let's keep at it and eventually arrive at the place of rest, not drop out through some sort of disobedience. — Message

Let us, therefore, make every effort to enter into that rest so that none of us fall through such disbelief as that of which we have had an example. — TCNT

I decree I am exerting myself and striving diligently to enter into God's place of rest. I decree I do not fall or perish by the same kind of unbelief or disobedience the children of Israel experienced in the wilderness.

August 10 – The Real Life

Keep yourselves in the love of God, looking for the mercy of our Lord Jesus Christ unto eternal life. Jude 21

Guard and keep yourselves in the love of God; expect and patiently wait for the mercy of our Lord Jesus Christ (the Messiah) - [which will bring you] unto life eternal. — Amp

Staying right at the center of God's love, keeping your arms open and outstretched, ready for the mercy of our Master, Jesus Christ. This is the unending life, the real life! — Message

And keep within the love of God while waiting for the mercy of our Lord Jesus Christ, to bring you to Immortal Life. — TCNT

Stay always within the boundaries where the love of God can reach and bless you. — Tay

I decree I am guarding my heart with all diligence, and I am keeping myself in the love of God. I decree I am waiting patiently and expectantly for the mercy of Jesus Christ to reach me and bless me, bringing me into eternal life, the real life!

August 11 – Blessed Memory

The memory of the just is blessed... Proverbs 10:7a

The memory of the [uncompromisingly] righteous is a blessing... — Amp

A good and honest life is a blessed memorial... — Message

The memory of the righteous yieldeth blessing... — Rhm

The memory of the righteous continues a blessing... — Ber

The memory of the just is blessed... — Sprl

The virtuous man is remembered with blessings... — Jerus

The memory of the upright is blessed... — Mof

The righteous are remembered in blessings... — NEB

I decree I am an uncompromisingly righteous child of God because I am in Christ Jesus. I decree He makes my memory a blessing and I remember all things.

August 12 – Patience Brings Promises

For we have need of patience, that, after ye have done the will of God, ye might receive the promise. Hebrews 10:36

For you have need of steadfast patience and endurance, so that you may perform and fully accomplish the will of God, and thus receive and carry away [and enjoy to the full] what is promised. — Amp

But you need to stick it out, staying with God's plan so you'll be there for the promised completion. — Message

You still have need of patient endurance...you may obtain the fulfillment of His promise. — TCNT

Steady patience is what you need...you may receive what you were promised. — Mof

So that, as the result of having done...you may receive the promised blessing. — Wey

I decree I am living with steadfast patience and endurance so I can perform and fully accomplish the will of God for my life. I decree I stick it out and stay with God's plan so that I receive all of His promises and enjoy them to the fullest.

August 13 – No Fear Here

And in nothing terrified by your adversaries: which is to them an evident token of perdition, but to you of salvation, and that of God. Philippians 1:28

And do not [for a minute] be frightened or intimidated in anything by your opponents and adversaries, for such [constancy and fearlessness] will be a clear sign (proof and seal) to them of [their impending] destruction, but [a sure token and evidence] of your deliverance and salvation, and that from God. — Amp

Your courage and unity will show them what they're up against; defeat for them, victory for you - and both because of God. — Message

Your fearlessness will be to them a sure token of impending destruction but to you it will be a sure token of your salvation – a token coming from God. — Wey

I decree I am full of courage and united with God. I decree I am not afraid or intimidated by my opponents or adversaries and their deeds. I decree my fearlessness is a clear sign of their destruction, and my deliverance given to me from God.

August 14 – We Are Glad

The Lord hath done great things for us; where-of we are glad. Psalm 126:3

The Lord has done great things for us! We are glad! — Amp

God was wonderful to us; we are one happy people. — Message

Yahweh hath done great things with us, We are full of joy! — Rhm

Yes, great things He had done for us, and we rejoiced at it! — Mof

What marvels indeed He did for us, and how overjoyed we were! — Jerus

I decree the Lord has done great and wonderful things for me. I decree I am full of joy and rejoicing in what He has done for me. I decree I am exceedingly happy.

August 15 – Faith In God's Power

That your faith should not stand in the wisdom of men, but in the power of God. 1 Corinthians 2:5

So that our faith might not rest in the wisdom of men (human philosophy), but in the power of God. — Amp

Which made it clear that your life of faith is a response of God's power, not to some fancy mental or emotional footwork by me or anyone else. — Message

Plainly God's purpose was that your faith should not rest upon man's cleverness but upon the power of God. — Phi

That your faith might have a foundation not in the wisdom of men. — Con

So that your faith should be based, not on the philosophy of man. — TCNT

I decree I am not putting my faith in human philosophy or the wisdom of men. I decree I am putting my faith in the power of God. I decree He never disappoints me or lets me down.

August 16 – Everlasting Covenant

But My kindness shall not depart from thee, neither shall the covenant of My peace be removed, saith the Lord that hath mercy on thee. Isaiah 54:10b

Yet My love and kindness shall not depart from you, nor shall My covenant of peace and completeness be removed, says the Lord, Who has compassion on you. — Amp

My love won't walk away from you, My covenant commitment of peace won't fall apart. The God who has compassion on you says so. — Message

Never shall My love leave you, My compact for your welfare shall stand firm; so promises the Eternal in His pity. — Mof

My love shall be immovable and never fail, and My covenant of the peace shall not be shaken. So says the Lord who take pity on you. — NEB

I decree the Lord is compassionate toward me. I decree His love and kindness for me will never depart from Him. I decree I will always walk in His covenant of peace because He will never remove it from me.

August 17 – Holy Ghost Teacher

But the Comforter, which is the Holy Ghost, whom the Father will send in My name, He shall teach you all things, and bring all things to your remembrance, whatsoever I have said unto you. John 14:26

But the Comforter (Counselor, Helper, Intercessor, Advocate, Strengthener, Standby), the Holy Spirit, Whom the Father will send in My name [in My place, to represent Me and act on My behalf], He will teach you all things. And He will cause you to recall (will remind you of, bring to your remembrance) everything I have told you. — Amp

The Friend, the Holy Spirit whom the Father will send at My request, will make everything plain to you. He will remind you of all the things I have told you. — Message

...He will teach you all things, and will recall to your minds all that I have said to you. — TCNT

I decree Holy Spirit is my Comforter, Helper, Counselor, Intercessor, Advocate, Standby, and Strengthener. I decree He teaches me all things and makes everything clear to me. I decree He brings everything God says to my remembrance.

August 18 – A Lavish Celebration

For our light affliction, which is but for a moment, worketh for us a far more exceeding and eternal weight of glory. 2 Corinthians 4:17

For our light, momentary affliction (this slight distress of the passing hour) is ever more and more abundantly preparing and producing and achieving for us an everlasting weight of glory [beyond all measure, excessively surpassing all comparisons and all calculations, a vast and transcendent glory and blessedness never to cease!]. — Amp

The hard times are small potatoes compared to the coming good times, the lavish celebration prepared for us. — Message

The light burden of our momentary trouble is preparing for us, in measure transcending thought, a weight of imperishable glory. — TCNT

The slight trouble of the passing hour results in a solid glory past all comparison. — Mof

I decree this slight, momentary affliction of trouble is passing away. I decree it is producing, preparing, and achieving an everlasting weight of glory beyond all measure and exceeding in comparison to the lavish party and good times to come.

August 19 – Trustworthy Keeper

Preserve me, O God: for in Thee do I put my trust. Psalm 16:1

Keep and protect me, O God, for in You I have found refuge and in You do I put my trust and hide myself. — Amp

Keep me safe, O God, I've run for dear life to You. — Message

Keep me safe, Lord; I put my trust in Thee. — Knox

Preserve me, O God; for in Thee do I take refuge. — ASV

Guard me, O God, for I have taken shelter in Thee. — Sprl

Keep me, O God, for in Thee have I found refuge. — NEB

I decree am putting my trust in God to keep me and protect me. I decree He is my Refuge, and I am hiding myself in Him.

August 20 – Every Good Gift

Every good gift and every perfect gift is from above, and cometh down from the Father of lights, with whom is no variableness, neither shadow of turning. James 1:17

Every good gift and every perfect (free, large, full) gift is from above; it comes down from the Father of all [that gives] light, in [the shining of] Whom there can be no variation [rising or setting] or shadow casts by His turning [as in an eclipse]. — Amp

Every desirable and beneficial gift comes out of heaven. The gifts are rivers of light cascading down from the Father of Light. There is nothing deceitful in God, nothing two-faced, nothing fickle. — Message

All good giving and every perfect gift comes from above... — NEB

...the Father of the heavenly lights who knows no change of rising or of setting who casts no shadow on the earth. — Mof

I decree I am receiving all of the good and perfect gifts Father God has planned and prepared for me. I decree He only has good things prepared for me because He is good, and He does not change.

August 21 – Witty Inventions

I wisdom dwell with prudence, and find out knowledge of witty inventions. Proverbs 8:12

I, Wisdom [from God], make prudence my dwelling, and I find out knowledge and discretion. — Amp

I am Lady Wisdom, and I live next to Sanity; Knowledge and Discretion live just down the street. — Message

I, wisdom, dwell in prudence, and find out the knowledge of wise counsels. — ABPS

I, wisdom, dwell with insight, I find out knowledge through deliberating. — Ber

I, Wisdom, dwell with experience, and judicious knowledge I attain. — NAB

What am I, the wisdom that speaks to you? To shrewdness I am a near neighbour, and I occupy myself with deep designs. — Knox

I decree God is giving me wisdom and prudence to find knowledge from wise counsel. I decree He gives me ideas and knowledge for witty inventions.

August 22 – Faith Works In Love

For in Jesus Christ neither circumcision availeth anything, nor uncircumcision; but faith which worketh by love. Galatians 5:6

For [if we are] in Christ Jesus, neither circumcision nor uncircumcision counts for anything, but only faith activated and energized and expressed and working through love. — Amp

For in Christ, neither our most conscientious religion nor disregard of religion amounts to anything. What matters is something far more interior: faith expressed in love. — Message

For in union with Christ Jesus, neither circumcision nor the want of it counts for anything, but only faith acting through love. — Gspd

Once we are in Christ, circumcision means nothing, and the want of it means nothing; the faith that finds its expression in love is all that matters. — Knox

I decree I am living my life in Jesus Christ. I decree I am walking in love toward all people because this is what counts for everything. I decree my faith is activated, energized, and expressed in love.

August 23 – I Am Anointed

The Spirit of the Lord God is upon me; because the Lord hath anointed me to preach good tidings unto the meek; He hath sent me to bind up the broken-hearted, to proclaim liberty to captives, and the opening of the prison to them that are bound. Isaiah 61:1

The Spirit of the Lord God is upon me, because the Lord has anointed and qualified me to preach the Gospel of good tidings to the meek, the poor, and afflicted. He has sent me to bind up and heal the brokenhearted, to proclaim liberty to the [physical and spiritual] captives and the opening of the prison and of the eyes to those who are bound. — Amp

The Spirit of God, the Master, is on me because God anointed me. He sent me to preach good news to the poor, heal the heart-broken, announce freedom to all captives, pardon all prisoners. — Message

I decree the Spirit of the Lord is upon me. I decree He has anointed me to preach the Gospel, the good news to the poor. I decree I am anointed to heal the broken-hearted, set the captives free, and open the eyes of those who are bound.

August 24 – Mighty Seed

His seed shall be mighty upon earth: the generation of the upright shall be blessed. Psalm 112:2

His [spiritual] offering shall be mighty upon earth; the generation of the upright shall be blessed. — Amp

Their children robust on the earth, and the homes of the upright - how blessed! — Message

Children of such a man will be powers on earth, descendants of the upright will always be blessed. — Jerus

His children shall be honored everywhere, for good men's sons have a special heritage. — Tay

I decree I am upright before the Lord. I decree my seed is mighty on the earth. I decree my children and their children's children are blessed because of my wise decisions. I decree they are doing the powerful works of God.

August 25 – Passionate Patience

And not only so, but we glory in tribulations also; knowing that tribulation worketh patience. Romans 5:3

Moreover [let us also be full of joy now!] let us exult and triumph in our troubles and rejoice in our sufferings, knowing that pressure and affliction and hardship produce patient and unswerving endurance. — Amp

There's more to come: we continue to shout our praise even when we're hemmed in with troubles, because we know how troubles can develop passionate patience in us. — Message

This doesn't mean, of course, that we have only a hope of future joys - we can be full of joy here and now even in our trials and troubles. — Phi

...but we triumph even in our troubles... — Mof

...produces endurance... — Gspd

I decree I am full of joy now as I am triumphing over trials and troubles in my life. I decree I am rejoicing in sufferings, because I know the pressure, afflictions, and hardships are developing and producing passionate, unwavering patience.

August 26 – The Good News

And Jesus went about all Galilee, teaching in their synagogues, and preaching the gospel of the kingdom, and healing all manner of sickness and all manner of disease among the people. Matthew 4:23

And He went about all Galilee, teaching in their synagogues and preaching the good news (Gospel) of the kingdom, and healing every disease and every weakness and infirmity among the people. — Amp

From there he went all over Galilee. He used synagogues for meeting places and taught people the truth of God. God's kingdom was His theme - that beginning right now they were under God's government, a good government! He also healed people of their diseases and of the bad effects of their bad lives. — Message

...proclaiming the good news of the kingdom and curing every kind of disease and every kind of sickness... — TCNT

I decree I am living under God's government, proclaiming the good news of His kingdom. I decree I am curing all kinds of diseases, sicknesses, or infirmities because I am doing greater works than Jesus.

August 27 – Run The Race

Wherefore seeing we also are compassed about with so great a cloud of witnesses, let us lay aside every weight, and the sin which doth so easily beset us, and let us run with patience the race that is set before us. Hebrews 12:1

...and let us run with patient endurance and steady and active persistence an appointed course of the race that is set before us. — Amp

Do you see what this means - all these pioneers who blazed the way, all these veterans cheering us on? It means we'd better get on with it. Strip down, start running - never quit! No extra spiritual fat, no parasitic sins. — Message

...and run with resolution the race... — NEB

...and run with courage the race... — Con

...let us keep on running in the way which is marked out for us. — Bas

I decree I am confessing every sin that hinders me. I decree I am letting them go. I decree I am patiently and courageously running my race set before me with enduring persistence as those who have gone before me are cheering me on.

August 28 – Build Yourself Up

But ye, beloved, building up yourselves on your most holy faith, praying in the Holy Ghost. Jude 1:20

But you, beloved, build yourselves up [founded] on your most holy faith [make progress, rise like an edifice higher and higher], praying in the Holy Spirit. — Amp

But you, dear friends, carefully build yourselves up in this most holy faith by praying in the Holy Spirit. — Message

Staying right at the center of God's love, keeping your arms open and outstretched, ready for the mercy of our Master, Jesus Christ. It is for you, beloved to make your most holy faith the foundation of your lives. — Knox

But you, My friends, must fortify yourselves in your most sacred faith, continue to pray in the power of the Holy Spirit. — NEB

I decree I am building myself up in my most Holy faith as I am praying in the Holy Spirit. I decree I am making progress in the spirit realm and rising higher and higher as I am releasing my faith to receive what I am praying out in the Spirit.

August 29 – Doers Of The Word

But be ye doers of the word, and not hearers only, deceiving your own selves. James 1:22

But be doers of the Word [obey the message], and not merely listeners to it, betraying yourselves [into deception by reasoning contrary to the truth]. — Amp

Don't fool yourself into thinking that you are a listener when you are anything but, letting the Word go in one ear and out the other. — Message

Act on the word instead of merely listening to it... — Mof

Put the message into practice, do not merely listen to it... — TCNT

Keep on obeying this message... — Wms

I decree I am doing the Word of God that I hear. I decree I am not just listening to the Word of God. I decree I am obeying the message, so I do not deceive myself.

August 30 – Nothing Separates You

Nor height, nor depth, nor any other creature, shall be able to separate us from the love of God, which is in Christ Jesus our Lord. Romans 8:39

Nor height nor depth, nor anything else in all creation will be able to separate us from the love of God which is in Christ Jesus our Lord. — Amp

None of these fazes us because Jesus loves us. I'm absolutely convinced that nothing - nothing living or dead, angelic or demonic, today or tomorrow, high or low, thinkable or unthinkable - absolutely nothing can get between us and God's love because of the way that Jesus our Master has embraced us. — Message

Neither the height above us nor the depth beneath us, nor any other created thing will be able to separate us from the love of God, which comes to us in Christ Jesus our Lord. — Knox

I decree I am loved by God. I decree nothing in this world, or the spiritual realm can come between Him and me to separate me from His love. I decree His love comes to me as the gift of an embrace from Jesus Christ's love.

August 31 – Yoke Up Equally

Be ye not unequally yoked together with un-believers: for what fellowship hath righteous-ness with unrighteousness? And what com-munion hath light with darkness? 2 Corinthi-ans 6:14

Do not be unequally yoked with unbelievers [do not make mismatched alliances with them or come under a different yoke with them, inconsistent with your faith]. For what partnership have right living and right stand-ing with God with iniquity and lawlessness? Or how can light have fellowship with darkness? — Amp

Don't become partners with those who reject God. How can you make a partnership out of right and wrong? That's not partnership; that's war. Is light best friends with dark? — Message

...avoid unsuitable connections with unbelievers... — Wey

...stop forming intimate and inconsistent relations with unbelievers... — Wms

I decree I am a child of God and the Kingdom of Light. I decree I am not yoking myself up to an unbeliever in any type of personal or business relationship. I decree I am not entering into a relationship with a person who is rejecting God or fellowshipping with darkness.

SEPTEMBER

*Sin is no
longer
your
master,
for
you no
longer
live
under the
requirements
of the
law.
Instead,
you
live
under
the freedom
of God's
grace.
Romans 6:14*

September 1 – Abundant Mercy

Blessed be the God and Father of our Lord Jesus Christ, which according to His abundant mercy hath begotten us again unto a lively hope by the resurrection of Jesus Christ from the dead. 1 Peter 1:3

Praised (honored, blessed) be the God and Father of our Lord Jesus Christ (the Messiah)! By His boundless mercy we have been born again to an ever living hope through the resurrection of Jesus Christ from the dead. — Amp

What a God we have! And how fortunate we are to have Him, this Father of our Master Jesus! Because Jesus was raised from the dead, we've been given a brand-new life and have everything to live for, including a future in heaven - and the future starts now! — Message

...who has, in His great mercy, through the resurrection of Jesus Christ from the dead, given us the new life of undying hope. — TCNT

I decree I am blessed to have Jesus as my Lord and Savior. I decree I am praising God and giving Him honor. I decree I am thankful for His boundless mercy because I now have a new life and everything to live for. I decree my exciting future begins today!

September 2 – Unceasing Mercy

O give thanks unto the Lord, for He is good, for His mercy endureth forever. Psalm 107:1

O give thanks to the Lord, for He is good; for His mercy and loving-kindness endure forever! — Amp

Oh, thank God - He's so good! His love never runs out. — Message

...for His steadfast love endures forever! — RSV

...For His lovingkindness endureth forever. — ASV

...His kindness never fails! — Mof

I decree I am continuously thanking the Lord for being so good to me. I decree His mercy and loving-kindness toward me endure forever and they never run out.

September 3 – The Temple Of God

Know ye not that ye are the temple of God, and that the Spirit of God dwelleth in you? 1 Corinthians 3:16

Do you not discern and understand that you [the whole church at Corinth] are God's temple (His sanctuary), and that God's Spirit has His permanent dwelling in you [to be at home in you, collectively as a church and also individually]? — Amp

You realize, don't you, that you are the temple of God, and God Himself is present in you? — Message

...God's temple and that you form a shrine wherein God's Spirit dwells? — Con

Do you not know that you are God's sanctuary? — Mon

...and that God's Spirit has His home in you? — TCNT

...has His permanent home in you? — Wms

God's Spirit makes His home in you? — Gspd

I decree I am discerning and understanding that I am God's temple, His sanctuary. I decree His Holy Spirit lives in me. I decree I am His permanent dwelling place, His home.

September 4 – Patient In Spirit

Better the end of a thing than the beginning thereof: and the patient in spirit is better than the proud in spirit. Ecclesiastes 7:8

Better is the end of a thing than the beginning of it and the patient in spirit is better than the proud in spirit. — Amp

Endings are better than beginnings. Sticking to it is better than standing out. — Message

I decree I am finishing the things I start. I decree I am sticking with every project I begin until I have completed every task. I decree I am being patient in my spirit, and I am not proud.

September 5 – Not Forsaken

Cast me not off in the time of old age; forsake me not when my strength falleth. Psalm 71:9

Cast me not off nor send me away in the time of old age; forsake me not when my strength is spent and my powers fail. — Amp

Don't turn me out to pasture when I am old or put me on the shelf when I can't pull my weight. — Message

Thou wilt not cast me off when oppressed with years, when my strength is consumed Thou will not forsake me. — Sprl

Do not give me up when I am old; be my help even when my strength is gone. — Bas

Do not reject me now I am old, nor desert me now my strength is failing. — Jerus

I decree I am continuing to draw near to God as I am getting older. I decree I believe He will never cast me away, leave me nor forsake me, even when I am old, and my strength is failing me.

September 6 – Power To Get Wealth

But thou shalt remember the Lord thy God: for it is He that giveth thee power to get wealth. Deuteronomy 8:18

But you shall [earnestly] remember the Lord your God, for it is He Who gives you power to get wealth that He may establish His covenant which He swore to your fathers, as it is this day. — Amp

Remember that God, your God, gave you the strength to produce all this wealth so as to confirm the covenant that He promised to your ancestors - as it is today. — Message

You must remember that it is the Lord your God who has been giving you power to gain wealth. — AAT

I decree God is giving me the power to create wealth so that He may establish His covenant with me which is the same covenant He promised to my ancestors. I decree I will always remember what He is doing for me.

September 7 – Chosen Beforehand

According as He hath chosen us in Him before the foundation of the world, that we should be holy and without blame before Him in love.
Ephesians 1:4

Even as [in His love] He chose us [actually picked us out for Himself as His own] in Christ before the foundation of the world, that we should be holy (consecrated and set apart for Him) and blameless in His sight, even above reproach, before Him in love. — Amp

Long before He laid down earth's foundations, He had us I mind, had settled on us as the focus of His love, to be made whole and holy by His love. — Message

For He chose us in our union with Christ before the creation of the universe that we might be holy and blameless in His sight, living in the spirit of love. — TCNT

I decree God chose me as His own child before the foundation of the world. I decree I am holy, consecrated and set apart for God. I decree I am blameless in His sight. I decree He made me to be in union with Christ Jesus and I am the focus of His love.

September 8 – Obey And Prosper

If they obey and serve Him, they shall spend their days in prosperity, and their years in pleasures. Job 36:11

If they obey and serve Him, they shall spend their days in prosperity and their years in pleasantness and joy. — Amp

If they obey and serve Him, they'll have a good, long life on easy street. — Message

If they listen and do as He says, their days end in happiness, and their closing years are full of ease. — Jerus

I decree I am obeying and serving God. I decree I am spending my days enjoying prosperity and all my years I am living in pleasantness and joy.

September 9 – Hidden Treasures

In Whom are hid all the treasures of wisdom and knowledge. Colossians 1:3

In Him all the treasures of [divine] wisdom (comprehensive insight into the ways and purposes of God) and [all the riches of spiritual] knowledge and enlightenment are stored up and lie hidden. — Amp

All the richest treasures of wisdom and knowledge are embedded in that mystery and nowhere else. And we've been shown the mystery. — Message

In Him all the treasures of wisdom and knowledge are stored up, hidden from view. — Wey

...all treasures of wisdom and knowledge are to be found. — Gspd

I decree I am in God. I decree all the treasures of His divine wisdom and comprehensive insight into His ways and purposes and the riches of His spiritual knowledge are set up and hidden for me not from me.

September 10 – His Great Power

And what is the exceeding greatness of His power to upward who believe, according to the working of His mighty power. Ephesians 1:19

And [so that you can know and understand] what is the immeasurable and unlimited and surpassing greatness of His power in and for us who believe, as demonstrated in the working of His mighty strength. — Amp

Grasp the immensity of this glorious way of life He has for Christians, oh, the utter extravagance of His work in us who trust Him - endless energy, boundless strength! — Message

And the transcendent greatness of the power which He is able to exercise in dealing with us who believe in Him. — TCNT

And what the transcendent greatness of His power in us believers, as seen in the working of His infinite might. — Wey

I decree I am knowing and understanding the immeasurable, unlimited, and surpassing greatness of God's power in me because I believe. I decree He is demonstrating His mighty strength and extravagant love for me. I decree He has a great and glorious life planned for me and I believe I am receiving this wonderful life now.

September 11 – No Weapon

No weapon that is formed against thee shall prosper; and every tongue that shall rise against thee in judgement thou shalt condemn. This is the heritage of the servants of the Lord, and their righteousness is of Me, saith the Lord. Isaiah 54:17

But no weapon that is formed against you shall prosper, and every tongue that shall rise against you in judgement you shall show to be in wrong. This [peace, righteousness, security, triumph over opposition] is the heritage of the servants of the Lord [those in whom the ideal Servant of the Lord is reproduced]; this is the righteousness or the vindication which they obtain from Me [this is that which I impart to them as their justification], says the Lord. — Amp

This is what God's servants can expect. I'll see to it that everything works out for the best. God's Decree. — Message

I decree no weapon formed against me shall prosper. I decree every tongue that rises up against me in judgement, I will show it to be wrong and condemned. I decree this triumph over opposition is my heritage and Jesus is my justification.

September 12 – Purged To Serve

How much more shall the Blood of Christ, who through the eternal Spirit offered Himself without spot to God, purge your conscience from dead works to serve the living God? Hebrews 9:14

How much more surely shall the Blood of Christ, Who by virtue of [His] eternal Spirit [His own preexistent divine personality] has offered Himself as an unblemished sacrifice to God, purify our consciences from dead works and lifeless observances to serve the [ever] living God? — Amp

Think how much more the Blood of Christ cleans up our whole lives, inside and out. Through the Spirit, Christ offered Himself as an unblemished sacrifice, freeing us from all those dead-end efforts to make ourselves respectable, so that we can live all out for God. — Message

I decree the Blood of Jesus cleanses me from all unrighteousness. I decree He is the pure sacrifice that cleanses me and frees me from all my sins and makes me fit for a life of service to God.

September 13 – Wholesome Words

But shun profane and vain babblings: for they will increase unto more ungodliness. 2 Timothy 2:16

But avoid all empty (vain, useless, idle) talk, for it will lead people into more and more ungodliness. — Amp

Stay clear of pious talk that is only talk. Words are not mere words, you know. If they're not backed by a godly life, they accumulate as poison in the soul. — Message

Continue shunning worldly, futile phrases for they lead on to a greater depth of godlessness. — Wms

But from irreligious and frivolous talk hold aloof for those who indulge in it will proceed from bad to worse in impiety. — Wey

But keep away from those unholy, empty discussions... — Ber

But stand aloof from godless and idle chatter... — Nor

I decree I am avoiding empty, idle talk because it leads to ungodliness. I decree I am not gossiping. I decree I am speaking faith-filled words that bring life to me and those around me.

September 14 – Don't Grieve God

And grieve not the Holy Spirit of God, whereby ye are sealed unto the day of redemption. Ephesians 4:30

And do not grieve the Holy Spirit of God [do not offend or vex or sadden Him], by Whom you were sealed (marked, branded as God's own, secured) for the day of redemption (of final deliverance through Christ from evil and the consequences of sin). — Amp

Don't grieve God. Don't break His heart. His Holy Spirit, moving and breathing in you, is the most intimate part of your life, making you fit for Himself. Don't take such a gift for granted. — Message

You must not offend God's Holy Spirit... — Gspd

For it is through the Spirit that God sealed you as His, against the Day of Redemption... — TCNT

I decree I am not grieving God's Holy Spirit or breaking His heart. I decree He is the most intimate part of my life. I decree He has already sealed me and delivered me from the consequences of sin. I decree He made me fit for Himself.

September 15 – Taste And See

O taste and see that the Lord is good: blessed is the man that trusteth in Him. Psalm 34:8

O taste and see that the Lord [our God] is good! Blessed (happy, fortunate, to be envied) is the man who trusts and takes refuge in Him. — Amp

Open your mouth and taste, open your eyes and see - how good God is. Blessed are you who run to Him. — Message

O taste and see that good is Yahweh - how happy the man who seeketh refuge in Him! — Rhm

Try the Eternal; you will find Him kind; happy the man who take shelter with Him! — Mof

I decree I am opening my mouth and my eyes to taste and see God's goodness to me. I decree I am blessed, happy, fortunate, and to be envied because I trust in and take refuge in God.

September 16 – Call Unto God

Call unto Me, and I will answer thee, and show thee great and mighty things which thou knowest not. Jeremiah 33:3

Call to Me and I will answer you and show you great and mighty things, fenced in and hidden, which you do not know (do not distinguish and recognize, have knowledge of and understand). — Amp

Call to Me and I will answer you. I'll tell you marvelous and wondrous things that you could never figure out on your own. — Message

Let your cry come to Me, and I will give you an answer, and let you see great things and secret things of which you had no knowledge. — Bas

I decree I am calling out to God, and He hears me. I decree He is answering me and showing me great and mighty things that I do not know, understand, or cannot figure out on my own.

September 17 – Redeemed

Christ hath redeemed us from the curse of the law, being made a curse for us: for it is written, Cursed is every one that hangeth on a tree. Galatians 3:13

Christ purchased our freedom [redeeming us] from the curse (doom) of the Law [and its condemnation] by [Himself] becoming a curse for us, for it is written [in the Scriptures], Cursed is everyone who hangs on a tree (is crucified). — Amp

Christ redeemed us from that self-defeating, cursed life by absorbing it completely into Himself. Do you remember the Scripture that says, "Cursed is everyone who hangs on a tree"? — Message

Christ ransomed us from the curse pronounced in the Law, by taking the curse on Himself for us, for Scripture says – Cursed is any one who is hanged on a tree. — TCNT

I decree I am redeemed from the curse of the Law. I decree Jesus purchased my freedom by taking the self-defeating, cursed life, completely into Himself when He died on the cross.

September 18 – Trusting In Him

Trust in Him at all times: ye people, pour out your heart before Him: God is a refuge for us. Selah. Psalm 62:8

Trust in, lean on, rely on, and have confidence in Him at all times, you people; pour out your hearts before Him. God is a refuge for us (a fortress and a high tower). Selah [pause, and calmly think of that]! — Amp

So trust Him absolutely, people; lay your lives on the line for Him. God is a safe place to be. — Message

Trust Him continually, all you nations; disclose the depth of your minds to Him. — Har

O my people, trust Him all the time. Pour out your longings before Him for He can help! — Tay

...for God is our hope. — PBV

I decree I am trusting in, relying on, and putting my confidence in God at all times. I decree I am pouring out my heart to Him because He is a safe place for me to be.

September 19 – Praise The Lord

Let every thing that hath breath praise the Lord. Praise ye the Lord. Psalm 150:6

Let everything that has breath and every breath of life praise the Lord! Praise the Lord! (Hallelujah!). — Amp

Let every living, breathing creature praise God! Hallelujah! — Message

Let every breathing thing praise Yah... — Rhm

Let everything that breathes praise the Lord! Hallelujah! — AAT

Let all breath praise Jah... — ABPS

I decree I am praising God with every breath I take. I decree He is so good to me. I decree I am praising the Lord! Hallelujah!

September 20 – A Glorious Finish

The glory of the latter house shall be greater than of the former, saith the Lord of hosts: and in the place will I give peace, saith the Lord of hosts. Haggai 2:9

The latter glory of this house [with its successor, to which Jesus came] shall be greater than the former, says the Lord of hosts; and in this place will I give peace and prosperity, says the Lord of hosts. — Amp

This Temple is going to end up far better than it started out, a glorious beginning but an even more glorious finish: a place in which I will hand out wholeness and holiness. Decree of God-of-the-Angel Armies. — Message

...In this place will I grant prosperity and peace. This is the very word of the Lord of Hosts. — NEB

I decree I am ending my earthly life far better than I started out. I decree I am receiving more of God's peace, more prosperity, and wholeness in my life.

September 21 – Shout In Triumph

Let them shout for joy, and be glad, that favour my righteous cause; yea, let them say continually, let the Lord be magnified, which hath pleasure in the prosperity of his servant. Psalm 35:27

Let those who favor my righteous cause and have pleasure in my uprightness shout for joy and be glad and say continually, Let the Lord be magnified, Who takes pleasure in the prosperity of His servant. — Amp

Let them have the last word - a glad shout! - and say, over and over and over, "God is great - everything works together for good for His servant." — Message

Let them shout in triumph and rejoice who are desiring my justification. — Rhm

Let those who desire my vindication shout for joy and be glad and say evermore, "Great is the Lord, who delights in the welfare of His servant!" — RSV

I decree I am favoring God's righteous cause. I decree I am shouting with great joy and a voice of triumph! I decree I am continuously saying, "Oh, magnify the Lord who delights in my prosperity."

September 22 – Faith Brings Life

For therein is the righteousness of God revealed from faith to faith: as it is written, the just shall live by faith. Romans 1:17

For in the Gospel a righteousness which God ascribes is revealed, both springing from faith and leading to faith [disclosed through the way of faith that arouses to more faith]. As it is written, the man who through faith is just and upright shall live and shall live by faith. — Amp

God's way of putting people right shows up in the acts of faith, confirming what Scripture has said all along; the person in right standing before God by trusting Him really lives. — Message

...resulting from faith and leading on to faith. Through faith the righteous man shall find Life. — TCNT

...the upright will have life because of His faith. — Gspd

I decree I am really living life because I am walking in faith. I decree I am in right standing with Father God and I am trusting Him. I decree I am continuously living by faith.

September 23 – Believe And Prosper

...Believe in the Lord your God, so shall ye be established; believe His prophets, so shall ye prosper. 2 Chronicles 20:20b

...believe in the Lord your God and you shall be established, believe and remain steadfast to His prophets and you shall prosper. — Amp

...Believe firmly in God, your God, and your lives will be firm! Believe in your prophets and you'll come out on top! — Message

...Trust in the Lord, your God, and you will be found firm... — NAB

...Hold firmly to your faith in the Lord your God and you will be upheld... — NEB

...Have faith in His prophets and all will go well for you. — Bas

...Have faith in His prophets and you will be successful. — Jerus

I decree I am believing in the Lord, and I am being established more and more. I decree I am believing the words of God's prophets, so I am succeeding and prospering.

September 24 – Redeemed By God

Blessed be the Lord God of Israel; for He hath visited and redeemed His people. Luke 1:68

Blessed (praised and extolled and thanked) be the Lord, the God of Israel, because He has come and brought deliverance and redemption to His people! — Amp

Blessed the Lord, the God of Israel; He came and set His people free. — Message

...has come to His people and made them free. — Bas

...has cared for His people, and wrought their redemption. — Mof

I decree I am blessing and praising my Lord God who is the God of Israel. I decree Jesus is continuously caring for me. I decree He is redeeming me, delivering me, and setting me gloriously free.

September 25 – Come Worship

O come, let us worship and bow down: let us kneel before the Lord our maker. Psalm 95:6

O come, let us worship and bow down, let us kneel before the Lord our Maker [in reverent praise and supplication]. — Amp

So come, let us worship; bow before Him, on your knees before God, who made us! — Message

O come, let us worship, and fall prostrate; let us bend the knee in the presence of Jehovah our Creator. — Sprl

Come, let us bow down in worship; let us kneel before the Lord who made us. — NAB

Come! Let us throw ourselves at His feet in homage, let us kneel before the Lord who made us. — NEB

I decree I am kneeling before God, who is my Lord. I decree I am worshipping Him. I decree I am bowing down before Him, the Creator of heaven and earth and everything in it, and I am praising Him.

September 26 – Set Apart For God

But know that the Lord hath set apart him that is godly for Himself; the Lord will hear when I call unto Him. Psalm 4:3

But know that the Lord has set apart for Himself [and given distinction to] him who is godly [the man of loving-kindness]. The Lord listens and heeds when I call to Him. — Amp

Look at this: look Who got picked by God! He listens the split second I call to Him. — Message

Know that the Lord does wonders for His faithful one. — NAB

Know this, Yahweh works wonders for those He loves. — Jerus

But know that the Lord hath set apart the godly man as His own. — JPS

The Eternal listens when I call to Him. — Mof

I decree I am set apart for God and His loving-kindness surrounds me. I decree when I call out to Him, He hears me, and He listens. I decree He answers me with great wonders and shows me wonderful favor.

September 27 – No Condemnation

There is therefore now no condemnation to them which are in Christ Jesus, who walk not after the flesh, but after the Spirit. Romans 8:1

Therefore, [there is] now no condemnation (no adjudging guilty of wrong) for those who are in Christ Jesus, who live [and] walk not after the dictates of the flesh, but after the dictates of the Spirit. — Amp

With the arrival of Jesus, the Messiah, that fateful dilemma is resolved. Those who enter into Christ's being-here-for-us no longer have to live under a continuous, low-lying black cloud. A new power is in operation. — Message

Thus there is no doom now for those who are... — Mof

So there is no condemnation any more for those who are in union with... — Gspd

The conclusion of the matter is this: there is no condemnation for those who are united with... — NEB

I decree I am living my life in Christ Jesus. I decree I am not living my life according to the dictates of my flesh. I decree I am free from the condemnation of the enemy. I decree I am living my life in the Spirit.

September 28 – Put On Love

And above all these things put on charity, which is the bond of perfectness. **Colossians 3:14**

And above all these [put on] love and enfold yourselves with the bond of perfectness [which binds everything together completely in ideal harmony]. — Amp

And regardless of what else you put on, wear love. It's your basic, all-purpose garment. Never be without it. — Message

And over all the rest put on the robe of love which binds together and completes the whole. — Con

And above all you must be loving for love is the link of the perfect life. — Mof

...which binds everything together in perfect harmony. — RSV

...for love is the golden chain of all the virtues. — Phi

I decree I am walking in God's love. I decree it binds me together with others in complete harmony. I decree I am never without love, and I love people wherever I go.

September 29 – Christ's Indwelling Word

Let the word of Christ dwell in you richly in all wisdom; teaching and admonishing one another in psalms and hymns and spiritual songs, singing with grace in your hearts to the Lord. Colossians 3:16

Let the word [spoken by] Christ (the Messiah) have its home [in your hearts and minds] and dwells in you in [all its] richness, as you teach and admonish and train one another in all insight and intelligence and wisdom [in spiritual things, and as you sing] psalms and hymns and spiritual songs, making melody to God with [His} grace in your hearts. — Amp

Let the Word of Christ - the Message - have the run of the house. Give it plenty of room in your lives. Instruct and direct one another using good common sense. And sing, sing your hearts out to God! — Message

I decree I am allowing God's word to dwell in my heart and mind richly with all wisdom as I teach, train, and admonish others with all insight and intelligence. I decree I am singing psalms, hymns, and spiritual songs to God.

September 30 – Healing Power

And great multitudes came unto Him, having with them those that were lame, blind, dumb, maimed, and many others, and cast them down at Jesus' feet; and He healed them. Matthew 15:30

And a great multitude came to Him, bringing with them the lame, the maimed, the blind, the dumb, and many others, and they put them down at His feet; and He cured them. — Amp

They came, tons of them, bringing along the paraplegic, the blind, the maimed, the mute - all sorts of people in need - the more or less threw them down at Jesus' feet to see what He would do with them. He healed them. — Message

I decree I am laying all my needs at the feet of Jesus right now. I decree whatever I need, Jesus has already provided it and healed me. I decree I am receiving my healing right now in Jesus Name.

OCTOBER

For the
Lord
Your
God
is
going
with
you!
He will
fight
for
you
against
your
enemies,
and He
will
give you
victory!
Deuteronomy 20:4

October 1 – Praise His Power

Be thou exalted, Lord, in thine own strength: so will we sing and praise Thy power. Psalm 21:13

Be exalted, Lord, in Your strength; we will sing and praise Your power. — Amp

Show your strength, God, so no one can miss it. We are out singing the good news! — Message

Exalt Thyself, Jehovah, in Thy strength... — ABPS

Stand high above us, Lord, in Thy protecting strength... — Knox

...we will sing, chant and praise of your might. — NAB

...we will sing and strike the harp to Thy power! — DeW

...with song and with string will we sound forth Thy power. — Rhm

...that we may sing and praise Your power. — Har

I decree I am singing and praising God for His mighty power manifesting in my life. I decree He is showing me His strength in a way that I cannot miss it.

October 2 – Keys Of The Kingdom

And I will give unto thee the keys of the king-dom of heaven: and whatsoever thou shalt bind on earth shall be bound in heaven: and whatsoever thou shalt loose on earth shall be loosed in heaven. Matthew 16:19

I will give you the keys of the kingdom of heaven; and whatever you bind (declare to be improper and unlawful) on earth must be what is already bound in heaven; and whatever you loose (declare lawful) on earth must be what is already loosed in heaven. — Amp

And that's not all. You will have complete and free access to God's kingdom, keys to open any and every door: no more barriers between heaven and earth, earth and heaven. As yes on earth is yes in heaven. A no on earth is a no in heaven. — Message

...the realm of heaven, whatever you prohibit on earth will be prohibited in heaven and whatever you permit on earth will be permitted in heaven. — Mof

I decree I have the keys to Heaven's Kingdom. I decree I am exercising my power and authority of binding and loosing things on earth, so they are lining up with heavenly things.

October 3 – Established Strong

But the God of all grace, who hath called us un-to His eternal glory by Christ Jesus, after that ye have suffered a while, make you perfect, stablish, and strengthen, settle you. 1 Peter 5:10

And after you have suffered a little while, the God of all grace [who imparts all blessing and favor], who has called you to His [own] eternal glory in Christ Jesus, will Himself complete and make you what you ought to be, establish and ground you securely, and strengthen, and settle you. — Amp

You're not the only ones plunged into these hard times. It's the same with Christians all over the world. So keep a firm grip on the faith. The suffering won't last forever. It won't be long before this generous God who has great plans for us in Christ - eternal and glorious plans they are! - will have you put together and on your feet for good. — Message

...will Himself, after your brief suffering, restore, establish, and strengthen you on a firm foundation. — NEB

I decree I am being strengthened, settled, made complete, and firmly established into what God has created me to be. I decree the suffering I am experiencing now will not last forever.

October 4 – He Took My Infirmity

That it might be fulfilled which was spoken by Esaias the prophet, saying, Himself took our infirmities, and bare our sicknesses. Matthew 8:17

And thus He fulfilled what was spoken by the prophet Isaiah, He Himself took [in order to carry away] our weaknesses and infirmities and bore away our diseases. — Amp

He fulfilled Isaiah's well-known sermon: He took our illnesses, He carried our diseases. — Message

In fulfillment of these words in the Prophet Isaiah, He took our infirmities on Himself, and bore the burden of our diseases. — TCNT

I decree I am totally healed. I decree Jesus has taken away all of my weaknesses and infirmities. I decree He carried away all my sicknesses and diseases.

October 5 – Overcoming Power

**Who is He that overcometh the world, but he that believeth that Jesus is the Son of God?
1 John 5:5**

Who is it that is victorious over [that conquers] the world but he who believes that Jesus is the Son of God [who adheres to, trust in, and relies on that fact]? — Amp

The person who wins out over the world's ways is simply the one who believes Jesus is the Son of God. — Message

...or who is victor over the world... — NEB

Who is the world's conqueror... — Mof

I decree I am overcoming and conquering this world. I decree I am living a victorious life because I believe Jesus is the Son of God. I decree I am trusting in, relying on, and adhering to the fact that I am the victor.

October 6 – Living Through Jesus

In this was manifested the love of God toward us, because that God sent His only begotten Son into the world, that we might live through Him. 1 John 4:9

In this the love of God was made manifest (displayed) where we are concerned; in that God sent His Son, the only begotten or unique [Son], into the world so that we might live through Him. — Amp

This is how God showed His love for us; God sent His only Son into the world so we might live through Him. — Message

In this the love of God has made manifest among us that God sent His only Son... — RSV

This is how the love of God has appeared to us... — Mof

God's love to us has been revealed in this way... — Gspd

...that we might find Life through Him. — TCNT

I decree I am living my life through and connected with Jesus who is the only begotten Son of God. I decree Jesus is showing His love for me as I live and find my life through Him.

October 7 – Payday Is Coming

Be ye strong therefore, and let not your hands be weak: for your work shall be rewarded.
2 Chronicles 15:7

Be strong, therefore, and let not your hands be weak and slack, for your work shall be rewarded. — Amp

But it's different with you: be strong. Take heart. Payday is coming! — Message

Ye therefore be strong, and let not your hands be slack, for there is a reward for your work. — Rhm

But now you must be strong and not let your courage fall; for your work will be rewarded. — NEB

I decree I am strong. I decree my hands are not weak or slack in anything I do. I decree I am being rewarded for all my efforts. I decree my payday is coming to me now.

October 8 – All Things Are Possible

And He said, the things which are impossible with men are possible with God. Luke 18:27

But He said, What is impossible with men is possible with God. — Amp

"No chance at all," Jesus said, "If you think you can pull it off by yourself. Every chance in the world if you trust God to do it." — Message

...what is impossible to man's power is possible to God. — Knox

...what men can't do God can do. — Beck

I decree I am not trying to do things in and of myself. I decree I am knowing the things that look impossible to me are totally possible when I am putting my trust in God to do it for me!

October 9 – Transcending Peace

And the peace of God, which passeth all understanding shall keep your hearts and minds through Christ Jesus. Philippians 4:7

And God's peace [shall be yours], that [tranquil state of a soul assured of its salvation through Christ, and so fearing nothing from God and being content with its earthly lot of whatever sort that is, that peace] which transcends all understanding shall garrison and mount guard over your hearts and minds in Christ Jesus. — Amp

Before you know it, a sense of God's wholeness, everything coming together for good, will come and settle you down. — Message

...which transcends all our powers of thought, will...be a garrison to guard your hearts and minds in Christ Jesus. — Wey

...that surpasses all your dreams. — Mof

...through your union with Christ Jesus...will guard your minds and thoughts. — Gspd

I decree I am living in God's peace. I decree His peace is my peace. I decree His peace guards my heart and mind and surpasses all my understanding. I decree His peace settles down my mind and my heart.

October 10 – Rejoice In Salvation

Notwithstanding in this rejoice not, that the spirits are subject unto to; but rather rejoice, because your names are written in heaven. Luke 10:20

Nevertheless, do not rejoice at this, that the spirits are subject to you, but rejoice that your names are enrolled in heaven. — Amp

All the same, the great triumph is not in your authority over evil, but in God's authority over you and presence with you. Not what you do for God but what God does for you – that's the agenda for rejoicing. — Message

However, the important thing is not that demons obey you, but that your names are registered as citizens of heaven. — Tay

Yet it is not your power over evil spirits which should give you joy. — Phi

I decree I am walking in my God-given power and authority over demons, and they obey me. I decree I am rejoicing even more in the fact that my name is written in Heaven, and I am a citizen of Heaven.

October 11 – Be Yet Wiser

Give instruction to a wise man, and he will be yet wiser: teach a just man, and he will increase in learning. Proverbs 9:9

Give instruction to a wise man and he will be yet wiser; teach a righteous man (one upright and in right standing with God) and he will increase in learning. — Amp

But if you correct those who care about life, that's different - they'll love you for it! Save your breath for the wise - they'll be wiser for it; tell good people what you know - they'll profit from it. — Message

Give teaching to a wise man and he will become wiser; give training to an upright man, and his learning will be increased. — Bas

Give to a wise man and he will be wiser still. Inform a righteous man and he will increase learning. — Rhm

Impart unto the wise, and they will be wiser yet; instruct the upright, and he acquireth more. — Sprl

I decree I am a wise man, and I am receiving instructions, so I become wiser. I decree I am a righteous man and am being taught so I am increasing in learning.

October 12 – Rescued From Distress

The righteous cry, and the Lord heareth, and delivereth them out of all their troubles. Psalm 34:17

When the righteous cry for help, the Lord hears, and delivers them out of all their distress and troubles. — Amp

Is anyone crying for help? God is listening, ready to rescue you. — Message

The righteous cry, and Jehovah heareth, and delivereth them out of all their distresses. — DeW

When the righteous cry for help, the Lord hears, and delivers them out of all their troubles. — RSV

I decree I am crying out to the Lord for help, and He hears me. I decree He delivers me and rescues me out of all my distresses and troubles.

October 13 – Ready To Respond

For the eyes of the Lord are over the righteous, and His ears are open unto their prayers: but the face of the Lord is against them that do evil.
1 Peter 3:12

For the eyes of the Lord are upon the righteous (those who are upright and in right standing with God), and His ears are attentive to their prayer. But the face of the Lord is against those who practice evil [to oppose them, to frustrate, and defeat them]. — Amp

God looks on all this with approval, listening and responding well in what He's asked; but He turns His back on those who do evil things. — Message

Because the eyes of the Lord are on upright men, and His ears listen to their pleading cries... — Wms

...And His ears are attentive to their prayers... — TCNT

I decree the eyes of the Lord are watching over me because I am in right standing with Him. I decree His ears are attentive when I pray, and He hears me. I decree He is ready to respond to my needs and He answers my prayers.

October 14 – Create A Clean Heart

Create in me a clean heart, O God; and renew a right spirit within me. Psalm 51:10

Create in me a clean heart, O God, and renew a right, persevering, and steadfast spirit within me. — Amp

God, make a fresh start in me, shape a Genesis week from the chaos of my life. — Message

...and put a new and right spirit within me — RSV

A pure heart create for me, O God! A steadfast spirit renew within me. — DeW

Produce in me a purified heart, my God; a new, unwavering attitude of mind. — Har

Create in me a new, clean heart, O God, filled with clean thoughts and right desires. — Tay

I decree God is creating a clean heart in me and bringing order to my chaos. I decree He is renewing a right, persevering, and steadfast spirit in me.

October 15 – Not Forsaken

I have been young, and now am old, yet have I not seen the righteous forsaken, nor his seed begging bread. Psalm 37:25

I have been young and now am old, yet have I not seen the [uncompromisingly] righteous forsaken or their seed begging bread. — Amp

I once was young, now I'm a graybeard - not once have I seen an abandoned believer, or his kids out roaming the streets. Every day he's out giving and lending, his children making him proud. — Message

Yet have I not seen the righteousness forsaken, nor his offspring begging for bread. — DeW

I never saw a virtuous man deserted or his descendants forced to beg their bread. — Jerus

I decree I was once young and now I am old, and I am the uncompromisingly righteous of God through Christ Jesus. I decree I will not be forsaken neither will my children ever have to beg for bread.

October 16 – Let God Be Magnified

Let all those that seek Thee rejoice and be glad in Thee: and let such as love Thy salvation say continually, Let God be magnified. Psalm 70:4

May all those who seek, inquire of and for You, and require You [as their vital need] rejoice and be glad in You; and may those who love Your salvation say continually, let God be magnified! — Amp

Let all those on the hunt for you sing and celebrate. — Message

But let all who seek Thee be jubilant and rejoice in Thee and let those who long for Thy saving help every cry, 'All glory to God!' — NEB

But fill the followers of God with joy! Let those who love your salvation exclaim, "What a wonderful God He is!" — Tay

I decree I am searching for you with my whole heart, Lord, and I am finding you. I decree I am so glad, and I am rejoicing in God and His salvation. I decree I am magnifying and glorifying God because He is so wonderful to me.

October 17 – Come Boldly

Let us therefore come boldly unto the throne of grace, that we may obtain mercy, and find grace to help in time of need. Hebrews 4:16

Let us then fearlessly and confidently and boldly draw near to the throne of grace (the throne of God's unmerited favor to us sinners), that we may receive mercy [for our failures] and find grace to help in good time for every need [appropriate help and well-timed help, coming just when we need it]. — Amp

So let's walk right up to Him and get what he is so ready to give. Take the mercy, accept the help. — Message

So let us continue coming with courage to the throne of God's unmerited favor to obtain His mercy and to find His spiritual strength to help us when we need it. — Wms

...that we might receive mercy for our failures. — Phi

...and in His grace find timely help. — NEB

I decree I am coming fearlessly, confidently, and boldly to the throne of grace and God's unmerited favor. I decree I am receiving mercy and grace for my failures in every time of need.

FAITH BUILDERS FOR VICTORIOUS LIVING

October 18 – Long Life Satisfaction

With long life will I satisfy him, and shew him My salvation. Psalm 91:16

With long life will I satisfy him and show him My salvation. — Amp

I'll give you a long life, give you a long drink of salvation! — Message

I will satisfy him with long life, and let him see My saving care. — Mof

He will have the satisfaction of a long life, and I shall let him participate in My salvation. — Har

I give them life, long and full, and show them how I can save. — Jerus

I decree God is satisfying me with a long, full life and He is showing me His salvation.

October 19 – Praise And Exalt Him

Oh, that men would praise the Lord for His goodness, and for His wonderful works to the children of men! Let them exalt Him also in the congregation of the people, and praise Him in the assembly of the elders. Psalm 107:31-32

Oh, that men would praise [and confess to] the Lord for His goodness and loving-kindness and His wonderful works to the children of men! Let them exalt Him also in the congregation of the people and praise Him in the company of the elders. — Amp

So thank God for His marvelous love, for His miracle mercy to the children he loves. Lift high your praises when the people assemble, shout Hallelujah when the elders meet! — Message

Let them extol His name, where the people gather, glorify Him where the elders sit in council. — Knox

I decree I am praising God and thanking Him for His goodness and marvelous love to me. I decree He has endless mercy toward me. I decree I am exalting His Name and praising Him wherever I go.

October 20 – A Rich Harvest

Thou crownest the year with Thy goodness; and Thy paths drop fatness. Psalm 65:11

You crown the year with Your bounty and goodness, and the tracks of Your [chariot wheels] drip with fatness. — Amp

Paint the wheat fields golden, Creation was made for this! — Message

Thou crownest the year with Thy goodness, and Thy footsteps are dropping with riches. — DeW

Thy bounty it is that crowns the year; where Thy feet have passed, the streams of plenty flows. — Knox

The year is crowned with the good you give; life-giving rain is dropping from your footsteps. — Bas

You have crowned the year with your bounty, and your paths overflow with a rich harvest. — NAB

I decree I am walking on paths that drip with fatness. I decree I am enjoying a year crowned with supernatural abundance and overflowing with a rich harvest of God's goodness.

October 21 – Overflow Blessings

Give, and it shall be given unto you; good measure, pressed down, and shaken together, and running over, shall men give into your bosom. For with the same measure that ye mete withal it shall be measured to you again. Luke 6:38

Give, and [gifts] will be given to you; good measure, pressed down, shaken together, and running over, will they pour into [the pouch formed by] the bosom [of your robe and used as a bag]. For with the measure you deal out [with the measure you used when you confer benefits on others], it will be measured back to you. — Amp

Give away your life; you'll find life given back, but not merely given back - given back with bonus and blessing. Giving, not getting, is the way. Generosity begets generosity. — Message

Give, and gifts will be yours... — Knox

For the measure you give will be the measure you get back... — RSV

I decree I am a generous giver. I decree I am receiving gifts from men that are returning to me as good measures, pressed down, shaken together, and running over because I am generous to others.

October 22 – Always Pray

And He spake a parable unto them to this end, that men ought always to pray and not to faint. Luke 18:1

Also [Jesus] told them a parable to the effect that they ought always to pray and not to turn coward (faint, lose heart, and give up). — Amp

Jesus told them a story showing that it was necessary for them to pray consistently and never quit. — Message

He gave them an illustration to show... — Gspd

...how necessary it is for people always to pray and never to give up. — Wms

...and not be faint-hearted. — Rhm

...and never despair. — TCNT

I decree I am praying consistently, and I am not turning into a coward. I decree I am never going to quit, lose heart, give up, enter into despair or become faint-hearted in my prayer life.

October 23 – Gracious Words

Let your speech be always with grace, seasoned with salt, that ye may know how ye ought to answer every man. Colossians 4:6

Let your speech at all times be gracious (pleasant and winsome), seasoned [as it were] with salt, [so that you may never be at a loss] to know how you ought to answer anyone [who puts a question to you]. — Amp

Be gracious in your speech. The goal is to bring out the best in others in a conversation, not put them down, not cut them out. — Message

Let your talk always have a saving salt of grace about it and learn how to answer any question put to you. — Mof

Always put your message attractively, and yet pointedly and be prepared to give every inquirer a fitting answer. — Gspd

I decree my words are gracious and pleasant to others. I decree my words are not condemning to others. I decree I am bringing out the best in others. I decree I am giving a fit word in due season when I speak.

October 24 – Strong In The Lord

Finally, my brethren, be strong in the Lord, and in the power of His might. Ephesians 6:10

In conclusion, be strong in the Lord [be empowered through your union with Him]; draw your strength from Him [that strength which His boundless might provides]. — Amp

And that about wraps it up. God is strong, and He wants you strong. — Message

Let your hearts be strengthened and in the conquering power. — Con

For the future, find strength in your union with the Lord and the power which comes from His might. — TCNT

I have no more to say, brethren, except this, draw your strength from the Lord, from that mastery which His power supplies. — Knox

I decree I am strong in the Lord and in the power of His might because I am in union with Him. I decree I am drawing my strength from His strength. I decree I am using His conquering power in my life to overcome.

October 25 – Adopted Into His Family

To the praise of the glory of His grace, wherein He hath made us accepted in the beloved. Ephesians 1:6

[So that we might be] to the praise and the commendation of His glorious grace (favor and mercy), which He so freely bestowed on us in the Beloved. — Amp

Long, long ago He decided to adopt us into His family through Jesus Christ. (What pleasure He took in planning this!). — Message

Thus He would manifest the splendour of that grace by which He has taken us into His favour in the person of His beloved Son. — Knox

That we might learn to praise the glorious generosity of His grace which has made us welcome in the everlasting love He bears toward the Beloved. — Phi

I decree I am accepted in the beloved by God's grace, favor, and mercy. I decree He loves me. I decree He took great pleasure in planning my adoption into His family through Jesus Christ long before I was born. I decree I am His son.

October 26 – Truth Sets You Free

And ye shall know the truth, and the truth shall make you free. John 8:32

And you will know the Truth, and the Truth will set you free. — Amp

Then you will experience for yourselves the truth, and the truth will free you. — Message

And you shall find out the truth... — TCNT

And you will have knowledge of what is true... — Bas

And you will understand the truth... — Mof

...and that very truth will make you free. — Lam

...and the truth will set you free. — Wms

I decree I am knowing and understanding the truth and the truth is setting me free.

October 27 – Wisdom From God

But of Him are ye in Christ Jesus, who of God is made unto us wisdom, and righteousness, and sanctification, and redemption. 1 Corinthians 1:30

But it is from Him that you have your life in Christ Jesus, Whom God made our Wisdom from God, [revealed to us a knowledge of the divine plan of salvation previously hidden, manifesting itself as] our Righteousness [thus making us upright and putting us in right standing with God], and our Consecration [making us pure and holy], and our Redemption [providing our ransom from eternal penalty for sin]. — Amp

Everything that we have - right thinking and right living, a clean slate and a fresh start - comes from God by way of Jesus Christ. — Message

But thanks to Him you are in Christ Jesus, He has become our wisdom from God. — Wey

I decree my life is in Jesus. I decree everything I have - wisdom, righteousness, right thinking, right living, consecration, a clean slate, and redemption - give me a fresh start, coming from God through His Son, Jesus.

October 28 – Victory By The Blood

And they overcame him by the Blood of the Lamb, and by the word of their testimony. Revelation 12:11

And they have overcome (conquered) him by means of the Blood of the Lamb and by the utterance of their testimony. — Amp

They defeated him through the Blood of the Lamb and the bold word of their witness. — Message

...because of the Blood...and because of the word of... — ASV

And they conquered him by the Blood of the Lamb... — Lam

...by means of the Blood of... — Ber

They defeated him by the Blood of the Lamb and by the preaching of the Word. — Nor

Their victory was due to the Blood of the Lamb, and the message to which they bore their testimony. — TCNT

I decree I am an overcomer, a conqueror. I decree I am conquering the devil and his demons by the Blood of the Lamb and the bold word of my testimony.

October 29 – God-Begotten Child

But as many as received Him, to them gave He power to become the sons of God, even to them that believe on His name. John 1:12

But to as many as did receive and welcome Him, He gave the authority (power, privilege, right) to become the children of God, that is, to those who believe in (adhere to, trust in, and rely on) His name. — Amp

But whoever did want Him, who believed He was who He claimed and would do what He said, He made to be their true selves, their child-of-God selves. These are the God-begotten not blood-begotten. — Message

...He empowered to become the children of God... — Knox

...to those who had faith in His name. — Bas

...to those who have yielded Him their allegiance. — NEB

I decree I have received Jesus and I am trusting in His Name. I decree I am believing in Him, adhering to, trusting in, and relying on His Name. I decree Jesus gives me His authority, power, and the privilege to become God's child.

October 30 – Richer And Richer

Then Isaac sowed in the land, and received in the same year an hundred-fold: and the Lord blessed him. Genesis 26:12

Then Isaac sowed seed in that land and received in the same year a hundred times as much as he had planted, and the Lord favored him with blessings. — Amp

Isaac planted crops in that land and took in a huge harvest. God blessed him. The man got richer and richer by the day until he was very wealthy. — Message

...hundredfold of barley... — Sept

I decree I am receiving a hundred-fold harvest on the seed I have sown this year. I decree God is favoring me with blessings and riches until I am very wealthy.

October 31 – Hold Fast Your Confession

Seeing then that we have a great high priest, that is passed into the heavens, Jesus the Son of God, let us hold fast our profession. Hebrews 4:14

Inasmuch as we have a great High Priest Who has [already] ascended and passed through the heavens, Jesus the Son of God, let us hold fast our confession [of faith in Him]. — Amp

Now that we know what we have - Jesus, this great High Priest with ready access to God - let's not let it slip through our fingers. — Message

Having then a great high priest who hath passed through the heavens, Jesus, let us hold fast our confession. — ASV

...let us continue to keep a firm hold on our profession of faith in Him. — Wms

...therefore let us never stop trusting Him. — Tay

I decree I am holding fast to my confession of faith, because Jesus is the great High Priest of my confession. I decree I am trusting Him because He went back to Heaven and sat down at the right hand of Father God.

NOVEMBER

*Give
thanks
to
the
Lord,
for
He is
good!
His
Faithful
love
endures
forever.*
1 Chronicles 16:34

November 1 – Love Your Enemies

But I say unto you, Love your enemies, bless them that curse you, do good to them that hate you, and pray for them which despitefully use you, and persecute you. Matthew 5:44

But I tell you, Love your enemies and pray for those who persecute you. — Amp

I'm telling you to love your enemies. Let them bring out the best in you, not the worst. When someone gives you a hard time, respond with the energies of prayer, for then you are working out of your true selves, your God-created selves. — Message

Love your enemies, and pray for them that persecute you. — ASV

...and pray for your persecutors. — Wey

...and make prayer for those who are cruel to you. — Bas

I decree I am loving my enemies. I decree I am blessing those that curse me, and I am doing good to those that hate me. I decree I am praying for the people that use me. I decree they are revealing my true self and they are seeing God's love in me.

November 2 – God's Greatest Love

For God so loved the world, that He gave His only begotten Son, that whosoever believeth in Him should not perish, but have everlasting life. John 3:16

For God so greatly loved and dearly prized the world that He [even] gave up His only begotten (unique) Son, so that whoever believes in (trusts in, clings to, relies on) Him shall not perish (come to destruction, be lost) but have eternal (everlasting) life. — Amp

This is how much God loved the world: He gave His Son, His one and only Son. And this is why: so that no one need be destroyed; by believing in Him, anyone can have a whole and lasting life. — Message

...had such love for the world... — Bas

...loved the world so dearly... — Mof

...whoever trusts in Him... — Mon

...so that no one who believes in Him should be lost. — Gspd

I decree I am so loved by God. I decree He sent His only Son to die for me. I decree I am believing in Him. I decree I am trusting in, clinging to, and relying on Him so I will have everlasting life with Him.

November 3 – Renewed Youth

Who satisfieth thy mouth with good things; so that thy youth is renewed like the eagle's. Psalm 103:5

Who satisfies your mouth [your necessity and desire at your personal age and situation] with good so that your youth, renewed, is like the eagle's [strong, overcoming, soaring]! — Amp

He renews your youth - you're always young in His presence. — Message

Who satisfieth thy desire with good things, so that thy youth is renewed like the eagle. — ASV

Who satisfies you with good as long as you live so that your youth is renewed like the eagle's. — RSV

I decree I am being satisfied with the good desires of my current age and situation. I decree my youthful strength is being renewed. I decree I am strong, soaring like the eagles.

November 4 – Ask In Jesus Name

And whatsoever ye shall ask in My name, that will I do, that the Father may be glorified in the Son. John 14:13

And I will do [I Myself will grant] whatever you ask in My Name [as presenting all that I AM], so that the Father may be glorified and extolled in (through) the Son. — Amp

From now on, whatever you request along the lines of who I am and what I am doing, I'll do it. That's how the Father will be seen for who He is in the Son. I mean it, whatever you request in this way, I'll do. — Message

...and I will do whatever you ask in My name... — Mof

...that the Son may bring glory to the Father... — Phi

...for this will bring praise to the Father because of what I, the Son, will do for you. — Tay

I decree I am asking God in Jesus' name for the desires of my heart. I decree I am knowing that He hears me and will do it for me so that God will be glorified in me through Jesus.

November 5 – Life-Long Praises

While I live will I praise the Lord: I will sing praises unto my God while I have any being. Psalm 146:2

While I live will I praise the Lord; I will sing praises to my God while I have any being. — Amp

All my life long I'll praise God, singing songs to my God as long as I live. — Message

I will praise Yahweh while I live! I will make melody to my God while I continue! — Rhm

I mean to praise Yahweh all my life. I mean to sing to my God as long as I live. — Jerus

I decree I am praising God. I decree I am singing His praises as long as I have breath in my body. I decree He is so good to me.

November 6 – More Than A Conqueror

Nay, in all these things we are more than conquerors through Him that loved us. Romans 8:37

Yet amid all these things we are more than conquerors and gain a surpassing victory through Him Who loved us. — Amp

None of this fazes us because Jesus loves us. — Message

Yet amidst all these things we more than conquer... — TCNT

And yet in all these things we keep on gloriously conquering... — Wms

No, in all these things we win an overwhelming victory through Him who has proved His love for us. — Phi

I decree I am more than a conqueror. I decree Jesus loves me so nothing I am going through fazes me. I decree God makes me more than a conqueror, and He is giving me overwhelming victory.

November 7 – Well And Whole

Peace I leave with you, My peace I give unto you: not as the world giveth, give unto you. Let not your heart be troubled, neither let it be afraid. John 14:27

Peace I leave with you; My [own] peace I now give and bequeath to you. Not as the world gives do I give to you. Do not let your hearts be troubled, neither let them be afraid. [Stop allowing yourselves to be agitated and disturbed; and do not permit yourselves to be fearful and intimidated and cowardly and unsettled.]. — Amp

I'm leaving you well and whole. That's My parting gift to you. Peace. I don't leave you the way you're used to being left - feeling abandoned, bereft. So don't be upset. Don't be distraught. — Message

...My gift is nothing like the peace of this world... — Phi

...Do not allow your hearts to be unsettled or intimidated. — Ber

I decree I am dwelling in the peace of God that Jesus gives me. I decree my heart is settled. I decree I am not fearful, intimidated, cowardly, disturbed, or agitated. I decree my heart is full of peace.

November 8 – Faith That Delivers

And Jesus said unto him, receive thy sight: thy faith hath saved thee. Luke 18:42

And Jesus said to him, Receive your sight! Your faith (your trust and confidence that spring from your faith in God) has healed you. — Amp

Jesus said, "Go ahead - see again! Your faith has saved and healed you! "The healing was instant. — Message

...your faith has delivered you. — TCNT

...your faith has cured you. — Wey

...your faith has brought thee recovery. — Knox

I decree faith is consuming me. I decree I am trusting God and put my confidence in Him. I decree I am believing I am receiving my salvation and healing right now according to my faith.

November 9 – Arise To A New Life

Arise, shine, for the light is come, and the glory of the Lord is risen upon thee. Isaiah 60:1

Arise [from the depression and prostration in which circumstances have kept you - rise to a new life]! Shine (be radiant with the glory of the Lord), for your light has come, and the glory of the Lord has risen upon you! — Amp

Get out of bed, Jerusalem! Wake up. Put your face in the sunlight. God's bright glory has risen for you. — Message

Arise, shine out, for your light has come, the glory of Yahweh is rising on you. — Jerus

Rise up in splendor! Your light has come, the glory of the Lord shines upon you. — NAB

I decree I am rising up from the depression and prostration of where circumstances have held me. I decree I am rising to a new life by changing my thoughts and attitude. I decree God's glory is upon me. I decree I am coming up higher in the things of God.

November 10 – See God's Glory

Jesus saith unto her, said I not unto thee, that, if thou wouldest believe, thou shouldest see the glory of God? John 11:40

Jesus said to her, did I not tell you and promise you that if you would believe and rely on Me, you would see the glory of God? — Amp

Jesus looked her in the eye. "Didn't I tell you that if you believed, you would see the glory of God?" — Message

...if you had faith... — Bas

...if you will only believe... — Mof

...thou will see God glorified. — Knox

...you would see the wonder of what God can do. — Phi

I decree I am believing in all the promises of God. I decree I am relying on Him, and I am seeing His glory manifested all around me. I decree I am seeing His promises for me fulfilled today.

November 11 – Stop Being Anxious

Fear thou not; for I am with thee: be not dismayed; for I am Thy God: I will strengthen thee; yea, I will help thee; yea, I will uphold thee with the right hand of My righteousness. Isaiah 41:10

Fear not [there is nothing to fear], for I am with you; do not look around you in terror and be dismayed, for I am your God. I will strengthen and harden you to difficulties, yes, I will help you; yes, I will hold you up and retain you with My [victorious] right hand of rightness and justice. — Amp

Don't panic, I'm with you. There's no need to fear for I'm your God. I'll give you strength, I'll help you. I'll hold you steady, keep a firm grip on you. — Message

Do not be afraid for I am with you; stop being anxious and watchful, for I am your God... — Jerus

I decree I am not being anxious, fretful, or fearful of anything because God is with me. I decree He is strengthening me and hardening me to difficulties. I decree He is helping me and holding me in His victorious right hand. I decree I am secure in His grip.

November 12 – Holy Ghost Baptism

Then remembered I the word of the Lord, how that He said, John indeed baptized with water; but ye shall be baptized with the Holy Ghost. Acts 11:16

Then I recalled the declaration of the Lord, how He said, John indeed baptized with water, but you shall be baptized with (be placed in, introduced into) the Holy Spirit. — Amp

I remembered Jesus' words: 'John baptized with water; you will be baptized with the Holy Spirit.' — Message

Then I remembered the Lord's words, how He said... — Wey

Then I was reminded of what the Lord said to us... — Knox

...in water...in the Holy Spirit. — Gspd

I decree I am baptized with water, and Holy Spirit's power with the evidence of speaking in other tongues. I decree He lives in me, and I let Him flow through me.

November 13 – Be Willing And Obedient

If ye be willing and obedient, ye shall eat the good of the land. Isaiah 1:19

If you are willing and obedient, you shall eat the good of the land. — Amp

If you'll willingly obey, you'll feast like kings. — Message

If ye be willing - and harken, of the good of the land shall ye eat. — Rhm

If you give ear to My word and do it, the good things of the land will be yours. — Bas

Obey with a will, and you shall eat the best that earth yields. — NEB

I decree I am humbling myself and submitting my will to God's will. I decree I am obeying His commands to prosper. I decree I am enjoying a king's feast from the land. I decree I am eating the best of what the earth yields.

November 14 – Completely Filled

Blessed are they which do hunger and thirst after righteousness: for they shall be filled. Matthew 5:6

Blessed and fortunate and happy and spiritually prosperous (in that state in which the born-again child of God enjoys His favor and salvation) are those who hunger and thirst for righteousness (uprightness and right standing with God), for they shall be completely satisfied! — Amp

You're blessed when you've worked up a good appetite for God. He's food and drink in the best meal you'll ever eat. — Message

Happy are those whose heart's desire is for righteousness... — Bas

...for being and doing right... — Wms

...completely satisfied. — Wey

I decree I am blessed - fortunate, happy, and spiritually prosperous - because I am a child of God. I decree I am enjoying His favor and my salvation. I decree I am hungry and thirsty for righteousness, and I am completely satisfied!

November 15 – Precious Thoughts

How precious also are Thy thoughts unto me, O God! How great is the sum of them! Psalm 139:17

How precious and weighty also are Your thoughts to me, O God! How vast is the sum of them! — Amp

Your thoughts - how rare, how beautiful! God, I'll never comprehend them! — Message

To me then how precious have Thy desires become O God! — Rhm

How weighty are your designs, O God! — NAB

How immeasurable Your concepts are, my God! — Har

God, how hard it is to grasp your thoughts! How impossible to count them! — Jerus

How deep I find Thy thoughts, O God! How inexhaustible their themes! — NEB

I decree God is always thinking about me. I decree His thoughts for me are weighty, immeasurable, beautiful, and precious. I decree I am overwhelmed by His great love for me. I decree I will never comprehend all of His thoughts.

November 16 – The Title Deed

Now faith is the substance of things hoped for, the evidence of things not seen. Hebrews 11:1

Now faith is the assurance (the confirmation, the title deed) of the things [we] hope for, being the proof of things [we] do not see and the conviction of their reality [faith perceiving as real fact what is not revealed to the senses]. — Amp

The fundamental fact of existence is that this trust in God, this faith, is the firm foundation under everything that makes life worth living. It's our handle on what we can't see. — Message

Now faith is the title-deed of things hoped for, the putting to the proof of things not seen. — Mon

And what is faith? Faith gives substance to our hopes... — NEB

I decree I am living with the Godkind of faith. I decree it is the firm foundation under everything that makes my life worth living. I decree I am full of faith. I decree I have the confident assurance or title-deed that says I have everything now that my heart is hoping for.

November 17 – Heart Thoughts

For as he thinketh in his heart, so is he... —
Proverbs 23:7a

For as he thinks in his heart, so is he... — Amp

He'll be stingy with you as he is with himself... — Message

For as he reckoneth within himself, so is he... — RV

For as he thinks in his soul, so is he... — ABPS

I decree I am thinking God's thoughts about myself and my situations. I decree He made me in the image and likeness of His Son, Jesus, and I am thinking like Jesus thinks.

November 18 – Angels On Guard

For He shall give His angels charge over thee, to keep thee in all thy ways. Psalm 91:11

For He will give His angels [especial] charge over you to accompany and defend and preserve you in all your ways [of obedience and service]. — Amp

He ordered His angels to guard you wherever you go. — Message

For His messengers will He charge concerning thee, to keep thee in all thy ways. — Rhm

For He puts you under His angels' charge, to guard you wherever you go. — Mof

For He gives His angels orders regarding you, to protect you wherever you go. — Ber

I decree my angel goes with me wherever I go. I decree I am charging him to watch over me and protect me wherever I go. I decree he is constantly guarding me in all my ways.

November 19 – Rejoice In The Lord

Yet I will rejoice in the Lord, I will joy in the God of my salvation. Habakkuk 3:18

Yet I will rejoice in the Lord; I will exult in the [victorious] God of my salvation! — Amp

I'm singing joyful praise to God. I'm turning cartwheels of joy to my Savior God. — Message

Yet I will exult in Jehovah, I will joy in the God of my deliverance. — ABPS

I decree I am singing joyful praises to God. I decree I am rejoicing in Him for He has given me my victorious salvation and deliverance.

November 20 – Possessing Authority

And God said, Let us make man in our image, after our likeness: and let them have dominion over the fish of the sea, and over the fowl of the air, and over the cattle, and over all the earth, and over every creeping thing that creepeth upon the earth. Genesis 1:26

God said, Let Us [Father, Son, and Holy Spirit] make mankind in Our image, after Our likeness, and let them have complete authority over the fish of the sea, the birds of the air, the [tame] beasts, and over all of the earth, and over everything that creeps upon the earth. — Amp

God spoke: "Let us make human beings in our image, make them reflecting our nature so they can be responsible for the fish in the sea, the birds in the air, the cattle, and yes, earth itself, and every animal that moves on the face of earth. — Message

I decree I am made in the image and likeness of God the Father, His Son Jesus, and Holy Spirit. I decree I have complete authority over everything on the earth. I am ruling and reigning in my domain.

November 21 – The Life-Giver

...for I am the Lord that healeth thee. Exodus 15:26b

...for I am the Lord Who heals you. — Amp

...I am God your healer. — Message

...for I, Jehovah, am healing thee. — YLT

...for I am Jehovah Thy physician. — Sprl

...for I am the Lord your life-giver. — Bas

...I am the Lord, and it is health I bring thee. — Knox

...for I, the Lord, make you immune to them. — AAT

I decree God is my Healer. I decree He is healing me right now and I receive my promise of healing into my body now. I decree no sickness can stay in my body. I decree God is my life-giver. I decree He makes me immune to sickness and disease.

November 22 – Unchangeable Jesus

Jesus Christ the same yesterday, and today and forever. Hebrews 13:8

Jesus Christ (the Messiah) is [always] the same, yesterday, today, [yes] and forever (to the ages). — Amp

For Jesus doesn't change - yesterday, today, tomorrow, He's always totally Himself. — Message

Jesus Christ is the same yesterday and today, yea and forever. — ASV

Jesus Christ is always the same... — Mof

What Jesus Christ was yesterday, and is today, He remains forever. — Knox

Jesus Christ is the same today that He was yesterday, and He will be so forever. — Gspd

I decree I am made in the image and likeness of Jesus. I decree He does not change from day to day, so I do not change from day to day. I decree in an ever-changing world, Jesus never changes. He is the same yesterday, today and tomorrow. He is stable so I decree I am stable.

November 23 – Faith Brings Healing

But when Jesus turned him about, and when He saw her, he said, daughter, be of good comfort; thy faith hath made thee whole. And the woman was made whole from that hour. Matthew 9:22

Jesus turned around and, seeing her, He said. Take courage, daughter! Your faith has made you well. And at once the woman was restored to health. — Amp

Jesus turned - caught her at it. Then He reassured her: "Courage, daughter. You took a risk of faith, and now you're well." The woman was well from then on. — Message

...thy faith hath brought thee healing... — Knox

...completely cured from that moment. — Phi

I decree Jesus is my Healer. I decree I am completely healed and made whole now. I decree I am walking in perfect health today. I decree my faith in God makes me well and Jesus is reassuring me that it is so. I decree it is done.

November 24 – Count It All Joy

My brethren, count it all joy when ye fall into diverse temptations; knowing this, that the trying of your faith worketh patience. James 1:2-3

Consider it wholly joyful, my brethren, whenever you are enveloped in or encounter trials of any sort or fall into various temptations. Be assured and understand that the trial and proving of your faith bring out endurance and steadfastness and patience. — Amp

Consider it a sheer gift, friends, when tests and challenges come at you from all sides. You know that under pressure, your faith-life is forced into the open and shows its true colors. So don't try to get out of anything prematurely. — Message

Reckon it nothing but joy when you find yourselves surrounded by various temptations... — Wey

...the testing of your faith develops endurance. — TCNT

I decree I am counting it all joy when I encounter various temptations and trials because I know my faith is being perfected. I decree they are bringing out my endurance, steadfastness and patience.

November 25 – Discover Real Life

For they are life unto those that find them, and health to all their flesh. Proverbs 4:22

For they are life to those who find them, healing and health to all their flesh. — Amp

Those who discover these words live, really live; body and soul, they're bursting with health. — Message

Keep these thoughts ever in mind; let them penetrate deep within your heart for they will mean real life for you, and radiant health. — Tay

Never lose sight of them, but fix them in your mind; to those who find them, they are life, and health to all their being. — Mof

Do not let them out of your sight, keep them deep in your heart. They are life to those who grasp them, health for the entire body. — Jerus

I decree I am finding and hiding God's Word in my heart. I decree I am meditating on His Words continually because they are giving me real life and producing radiant health for my entire body.

November 26 – Better Than Rubies

For wisdom is better than rubies; and all the things that may be desired are not to be compared to it. Proverbs 8:11

For skillful and godly Wisdom is better than rubies or pearls, and all the things that may be desired are not to be compared to it. — Amp

For wisdom is better than all the trappings of wealth; nothing you could wish for holds a candle to her. — Message

For better is wisdom than rubies, Yea, all delights are not comparable with it. — YLT

For better is wisdom than ornaments of coral, and no delightful things can equal her. — Rhm

For wisdom is more precious than pearls, and nothing else is so worthy of desire. — Jerus

For wisdom is better than rubies, no treasure is equal to her. — Mof

I decree I am hungering for and seeking after God's wisdom. I decree it is better than rubies or pearls. I decree I am full of God's wisdom because nothing compares to His wisdom.

November 27 – Greater And Mightier

Ye are of God, little children, and have over-come them; because greater is He that is in you, than he that is in the world. 1 John 4:4

Little children, you are of God [you belong to Him] and have [already] defeated and overcome them [the agents of the antichrist], because He Who lives in you is greater [mightier] than he who is in the world. — Amp

My dear children, you come from God and belong to God. You have already won a big victory over those false teachers, for the Spirit in you is far stronger than anything in the world. — Message

But you, My children, are of God's family and you have the mastery over these false prophets...— NEB

I decree I am God's child and I belong to Him. I decree I have already defeated and overcome Satan and his demons because God is greater than the enemy forces that are in this world. I decree I am an overcomer, and I am walking in victory.

November 28 – Confident Trust

And He said unto her, daughter, be of good comfort: thy faith hath made thee whole; go in peace. Luke 8:48

And He said to her, Daughter, your faith (your confidence and trust in Me) has made you well! Go (enter) into peace (untroubled, undisturbed well-being). — Amp

Jesus said, "Daughter, you took a risk trusting Me, and now you're healed and whole. Live well, live blessed!" — Message

Daughter, cheer up! Your faith has healed you... — Ber

...it is your faith which has healed you... — Phi

I decree I am putting my faith, my confidence, and my trust in Jesus to be my Healer. I decree He is making me well and I receive my healing right now. I decree I am not troubled or disturbed, I decree I am entering into His peace.

November 29 – Seek God's Kingdom

But seek ye first the kingdom of God, and His righteousness; and all these things shall be added unto you. Matthew 6:33

But seek (aim at and strive after) first of all His kingdom and His righteousness (His way of doing and being right), and then all these things taken together will be given you besides. — Amp

Steep your life in God-reality; God-initiative, God-provisions. Don't worry about missing out. You'll find all your everyday human concerns will be met. — Message

Set your heart on His kingdom and all these things will come to you as a matter of course. — Phi

But you must make His kingdom and uprightness before Him, your greatest care. — Gspd

I decree I am seeking after and striving after God's Kingdom and His way of doing things. I decree I know the things I want will be added to me and come to me.

November 30 – Blood Sacrifice

Much more then, being now justified by His Blood, we shall be saved from wrath through Him. Romans 5:9

Therefore, since we are now justified (acquitted, made righteous, and brought into right relationship with God) by Christ's Blood, how much more [certain is it that] we shall be saved by Him from the indignation and wrath of God. — Amp

Now that we are set right with God by means of this sacrificial death, the consummate Blood sacrifice, there is no longer a question of being at odds with God in any way. — Message

Much more, then now that we have been pronounced righteous by virtue of the shedding of His Blood. — TCNT

...shall we be saved through Him from the wrath [to come]. — Alf

It is far more certain that through Him we shall be saved from God's anger. — Gspd

I decree I am justified, just as if I have never sinned. I decree I am the righteousness of God, in right standing with Him, because Jesus shed His precious Blood for me.

DECEMBER

*Declaring the
end and
the result
from the
beginning,
and from
ancient
times the
things which
have not
[yet] been
done, saying,
'My purpose
will be
established,
and I will do
all that
pleases Me
and
fulfills My
purpose.'
Isaiah 46:10*

December 1 – Wonder-Working God

Blessed be the Lord God, the God of Israel, who only doeth wondrous things. Psalm 72:18

Blessed be the Lord God, the God of Israel, Who alone does wondrous things! — Amp

Blessed God, Israel's God, the one and only wonder-working God! — Message

Blessed be Jehovah God, the God of Israel. Who alone doeth wonders. — ABPS

Blessed be Yahweh, the God of Israel, who alone performs these marvels! — Jerus

Blessed be the Lord God of Israel, who does wonderful deeds as none else. — Knox

Praise be to the Lord God, the God of Israel, the only doer of wonders. — Bas

I decree I am blessing the Lord. I decree I am praising Him and lifting His Name on high. I decree He does wondrous things for me.

December 2 – Poppy Seed Faith

And Jesus said unto them, because of your unbelief: for verily I say unto you, If ye have faith as a grain of mustard seed, ye shall say unto this mountain, remove hence to yonder place; and it shall remove; and nothing shall be impossible unto you. Matthew 17:20

He said to them, because of the littleness of your faith [that is, your lack of firmly relying trust], for truly I say to you, if you have faith [that is living] like a grain of mustard seed, you can say to this mountain, Move from here to yonder place, and it will move; and nothing will be impossible to you. — Amp

"Because you're not yet taking God seriously," said Jesus; "The simple truth is that if you had a mere kernel of faith, a poppy seed, say, you would tell this mountain, "Move! and it would move. There is nothing you wouldn't be able to tackle." — Message

I decree I am firmly relying on and trusting God. I decree I have faith as a grain of mustard seed, and it is producing mountain-moving results in my life. I decree nothing is impossible to me because I use my faith.

December 3 – A Sheltering Haven

I will say of the Lord, He is my Refuge and my Fortress: my God; in Him will I trust. Psalm 91:2

I say of the Lord, He is my Refuge and my Fortress, my God; on Him I lean and rely, and in Him I [confidently] trust! — Amp

Say this: "God, you're my Refuge. I trust in you and I'm safe!" — Message

I will say to Jehovah, O my Refuge and Fortress. Thou art my God, in whom I will trust. — DeW

Says of the Lord, "My Refuge and my Fortress. My God, in whom I trust." — AAT

I will say of the Lord. "You are my Sheltering Haven; my God whom I trust. — Har

I decree I am putting my trust in the Lord. I decree He is my Refuge, my Fortress, my Sheltering Haven.

December 4 – Energizing Strength

He giveth power to the faint; and to them that have no might He increaseth strength. Isaiah 40:29

He gives power to the faint and weary, and to him who has no might He increases strength [causing it to multiply and making it to abound]. — Amp

He energizes those who get tired, gives fresh strength to dropouts. — Message

He gives vigor to the weary; and to the powerless He increases strength. — ABPS

Into the weary He puts power, and adds new strength to the weak. — Mof

He gives power to the tired and worn out, and strength to the weak. — Tay

I decree I am overcoming being weary, weak, and worn out. I decree God is increasing my strength and causing it to abound. I decree when I feel weak or faint, He strengthens me.

December 5 – Powerful Words

So shall My word be that goeth forth out of My mouth: It shall not return unto Me void, but it shall accomplish that which I please, and it shall prosper in the things whereto I sent it. Isaiah 55:11

So shall My word be that goes forth out of My mouth: it shall not return to Me void [without producing any effect, useless], but it shall accomplish that which I please and purpose, and it shall prosper in the thing for which I sent it. — Amp

So will the words that come out of My mouth not come back empty-handed. They'll dot the work I sent them to do, they'll complete the assignment I gave them. — Message

...so the word that goes from My mouth does not return to Me empty, without carrying out My will and succeeding in what it was sent to do. — Jerus

I decree I am speaking life-giving words. I decree my words have creative power and they do not return to me void without producing an effect to where I send them. I decree my words accomplish what I am sending them out to do.

December 6 – Unbelievable Inheritance

The Spirit itself beareth witness with our spirit, that we are the children of God: and if children, then heirs; heirs of God, and joint heirs with Christ. Romans 8:16-17

The Spirit Himself [thus] testifies together with our own spirit, [assuring us] that we are children of God. And if we are [His] children, then we are [His] heirs also; heirs of God and fellow heirs with Christ [sharing His inheritance with Him]. — Amp

God's Spirit touches our spirits and confirms who we really are. We know who He is, and we know who we are: Father and children. And we know we are going to get what's coming to us - an unbelievable inheritance! — Message

The Spirit Himself endorses our inward conviction. If we are His children we share His treasures, and all that Christ claims as His will belong to all of us as well! — Phi

I decree Holy Spirit is testifying to my spirit and assuring me that I am God's child. I decree I am His heir, and a joint heir with Jesus. I decree I am sharing in an unbelievable inheritance that belongs to me because of His Covenant with me.

December 7 – Stand The Test

Blessed is the man that endureth temptation: for when he is tried, he shall receive the crown of life, which the Lord hath promised to them that love Him. James 1:12

Blessed (happy, to be envied) is the man who is patient under trial and stands up under temptation, for when he has stood the test and been approved, he will receive [the victor's] crown of life which God has promised to those who love Him. — Amp

Anyone who meets a testing challenge head-on and manages to stick it out is mighty fortunate. For such persons loyally in love with God, the reward is life and more life. — Message

...perseveres under trial... — NASB

...for once his testing is complete... — Phi

...which God has promised to those that love Him. — RSV

I decree I am blessed, happy and to be envied because I am persevering under trials and standing up under temptations. I decree I am patiently sticking it out and I am being approved. I decree I am receiving the victor's crown and my reward is an abundant, victorious life.

December 8 – Believe And Receive

And all things, whatsoever ye shall ask in prayer, believing ye shall receive. Matthew 21:22

And whatever you ask for in prayer, having faith and [really] believing, you will receive. — Amp

Absolutely everything, ranging from small to large, as you make it a part of your believing prayer, gets included as you lay hold of God. — Message

And whatever you ask in prayer, you will receive, if you have faith. — RSV

Anything you ask for in prayer, believe, and you will get it. — Beck

I decree I am praying and asking God in faith for what my heart desires. I decree I am believing and I am receiving the answers to my prayers when I make my requests known to God.

December 9 – Strengthen My Soul

In the day when I cried Thou answered me, and strengthened me with strength in my soul. Psalm 138:3

In the day when I called, You answered me; and You strengthened me with strength (might and inflexibility to temptation) in my inner self. — Amp

The moment I called out, You stepped in; You made my life large with strength. — Message

In the day I cried unto Thee then didst thou answer me. And didst excite me in my soul mightily. — Rhm

In the day when I called, then Thou didst answer me, didst embolden me with strength in my soul. — ABPS

On the occasion when I called You answered me and bolstered my morale greatly. — Har

I decree I am calling out to God, and He is answering me. I decree He is strengthening me with might and inflexibility to temptation in my soul. I decree He is greatly bolstering my morale.

December 10 – Awakened Faith

So then faith cometh by hearing, and hearing by the word of God. Romans 10:17

So faith comes by hearing [what is told], and what is heard comes by the preaching [of the message that came from the lips] of Christ (the Messiah Himself). — Amp

The point is, before you trust, you have to listen. But unless Christ's Word is preached, there's nothing to listen to. — Message

So faith comes from hearing what is told and that hearing comes through the message about Christ. — Gspd

We conclude that faith is awakened by the message. — NEB

...and the message is the word of Christ. — Phi

I decree my faith is being awakened. I decree my faith is strong and powerful because I am hearing God's Word preached. I decree I am continuously hearing God's Word and I am meditating on it.

December 11 – Be Content

Let your conversation be without covetousness; and be content with such things as ye have: for He hath said, I will never leave thee, nor forsake thee. Hebrews 13:5

Let your character or moral disposition be free from love of money [including greed, avarice, lust, and craving for earthly possessions] and be satisfied with your present [circumstances and with what you have]; for He [God] Himself has said, I will not in any way fail you nor give you up nor leave you without support. [I will] not, [I will] not, [I will] not in any degree leave you helpless nor forsake nor let [you] down (relax My hold on you)! [Assuredly not!]. — Amp

Don't be obsessed with getting more material things. Be relaxed with what you have. Since God assured us, "I'll never let you down, never walk off and leave you." — Message

I decree I am living my life being content with what I have. I decree I am free from the love of money, greed, lust, cravings for earthly possessions or material things. I decree I am satisfied with what I have. I decree God is never going to leave me, let me down, or forsake me. I decree He will not leave me helpless or relax His grip on me.

December 12 – Anything Can Happen

Jesus said unto him, If thou canst believe, all things are possible to him that believeth. **Mark 9:22**

And Jesus said, [You say to Me], If You can do anything? [Why,] all things can be (are possible) to him who believes! — Amp

Jesus said, "If? There are no 'ifs' among believers. Anything can happen." — Message

If there is anything I can do! Everything is possible for one who has faith. — Gspd

Anything can be done for one... — Mof

I decree I am believing in Jesus and the power He has given me through believing in Him. I decree all things are possible for me because I am using my faith. I decree I can do anything through my faith and believing that it is possible through Jesus.

December 13 – Unbelievable Benefits

But it is written, eye hath not seen, nor ear heard, neither have entered into the heart of man, the things which God hath prepared for them that love Him. 1 Corinthians 2:9

But on the contrary, as the Scripture says, what eye has not seen and ear has not heard and has not entered into the heart of man, [all that] God has prepared (made and keeps ready) for those who love Him [who hold Him in affectionate reverence, promptly obeying Him and gratefully recognizing the benefits He has bestowed]. — Amp

That's why we have this scripture text: no one's ever seen or heard anything like this, never so much as imagined anything quite like it - what God has arranged for those who love Him. — Message

...things which eye saw not... — ASV

...things beyond our hearing, things beyond our imagining... — NEB

I decree I am believing God for the things that are beyond my wildest imagination. I decree the Lord has unbelievable blessings in store for me to enjoy and I receive them now.

December 14 – No Anxieties

And the cares of this world, and the deceitfulness of riches, and the lusts of other things entering in, choke the word, and it becometh unfruitful. Mark 4:19

Then the cares and anxieties of the world and distractions of the age, and the pleasure and delight and false glamour and deceitfulness of riches, and the craving and passionate desire for other things creep in and choke and suffocate the Word, and it becomes fruitless. — Amp

Are overwhelmed with worries about all the things they have to do and all the things they want to get. The stress strangles what they heard, and nothing comes of it. — Message

The deceiving pleasures of being rich... — Wms

And the desires for other things enter in... — NASB

And it yields nothing... — Gspd

I decree I am laying aside all of the cares, worries, stress, distractions, and anxieties of this world so the Word of God can grow in my heart. I decree it produces fruit in my life.

December 15 – Encourage Yourself

He that speaketh in an unknown tongue edifieth himself; but he that prophesieth edifieth the church. 1 Corinthians 14:4

He who speaks in a [strange] tongue edifies and improves himself, but he who prophesies [interpreting the divine will and purpose and teaching with inspiration] edifies and improves the church and promotes growth [in Christian wisdom, piety, holiness, and happiness]. — Amp

The one who prays using a private "prayer language" certainly gets a lot out of it, but proclaiming God's truth to the church in its common language brings the whole church into growth and strength. — Message

When you talk a strange language, you encourage yourself, but when you speak God's Word, you help the church grow. — Beck

...may strengthen his own faith... — Knox

I decree I am praying in tongues, edifying, and encouraging myself and building up my most holy faith. I decree I am proclaiming God's truth to the church as I am edifying and promoting spiritual growth and strength in wisdom, piety, holiness, and happiness.

December 16 – A Fortunate Man

Praise ye the Lord. Blessed is the man that feareth the Lord, and delighteth greatly in His commandments. Psalm 112:1

Praise the Lord! (Hallelujah!) Blessed (happy, fortunate, to be envied) is the man who fears (reveres and worships) the Lord, who delights greatly in His commandments. — Amp

Hallelujah! Blessed man, blessed woman, who fear God, Who cherish and relish His commandments. — Message

How happy is the man who revereth Yahweh. In His commandments delighteth he greatly. — Rhm

O the blessedness of the man that feareth Jehovah; that delighteth greatly in His commandments! — DeW

Happy the man who fears Yahweh by joyfully keeping His commandments. — Jerus

I decree I am praising the Lord! I decree I am blessed, happy, fortunate, and to be envied because I fear, revere, and worship the Lord. I decree I am delighting myself in cherishing and keeping His commandments.

December 17 – None Like God

All my bones shall say, Lord, who is like unto Thee, which deliverest the poor from him that is too strong for him, yea, the poor and the needy from him that spoileth him? Psalm 35:10

All my bones shall say, Lord, who is like You, You Who deliver the poor and the afflicted from him who is too strong for him, yes, the poor and the needy from him who snatches away has goods? — Amp

Every bone in my body laughing, singing, "God, there's no one like you. You put the down-and-out on their feet and protect the unprotected from bullies!" — Message

This is the cry of my whole being. There is none like Thee, Lord, who else rescues the afflicted from the hand of tyranny, and the poor, the destitute, from his oppressors. — Knox

I decree I am laughing, singing, and rejoicing as I praise God because there is no one like Him. I decree my whole being is praising God because He rescues the afflicted from the hands of tyranny. I decree He delivers the poor and the destitute from their oppressors.

December 18 – Keep God's Company

Delight thyself also in the Lord; and He shall give thee the desires of thine heart. Psalm 37:4

Delight yourself also in the Lord, and He will give you the desires and secret petitions of your heart. — Amp

Keep company with God, get in on the best. — Message

Yea rest thy delight on Yahweh, that He may give thee the requests of thy heart. — Rhm

See thy pleasure in Jehovah. And He will give thee thy heart's desire. — DeW

Make Yahweh your only joy and He will give you what your heart desires. — Jerus

I decree I am delighting myself in the Lord and keeping company with Him. I decree He is giving me the very best He has as well as giving me the desires of my heart.

December 19 – Sons Through Faith

For ye are all the children of God by faith in Christ Jesus. Galatians 3:26

For in Christ Jesus you are all sons of God through faith. — Amp

By faith in Christ you are in direct relationship with God. — Message

For in Christ Jesus you are all sons of God through your faith. — Gspd

For now that you have faith in Christ Jesus you are all sons of God. — Phi

I decree I am living my life by putting my faith in Christ Jesus. I decree our relationship puts me directly into a relationship with Father God. I decree I am His son.

December 20 – Faith Pleases God

But without faith it is impossible to please Him: for He that cometh to God must believe that He is, and that He is a rewarder of them that diligently seek Him. Hebrews 11:6

But without faith it is impossible to please and be satisfactory to Him. For whoever would come near to God must [necessarily] believe that God exists and that He is the rewarder of those who earnestly and diligently seek Him [out]. — Amp

It's impossible to please God apart from faith. And why? Because anyone who wants to approach God must believe both that He exists and that He cares enough to respond to those who seek Him. — Message

You can never please God without faith, without depending on Him, and that He will reveal Himself to those who sincerely look for Him. — Tay

...for anyone who approaches God must believe... — Wms

I decree I am living a lifestyle of faith which is pleasing to God. I decree I am drawing near to God because I believe He exists. I decree He loves me and rewards me for earnestly and diligently seeking Him.

December 21 – Run To Peace

Follow peace with all men, and holiness, without which no man shall see the Lord. Hebrews 12:14

Strive to live at peace with everybody and pursue that consecration and holiness without which no one will [ever] see the Lord. — Amp

Work at getting along with each other and with God. Otherwise you'll never get so much as a glimpse of God. — Message

Run swiftly after peace with all men... — Mon

Try earnestly to live at peace with everyone and to attain to that purity without which... — TCNT

Let it be your ambition to live at peace... — Tay

And strive for that consecration without which no one can see... — Gspd

I decree I am living in peace with God and everyone around me. I decree I am pursuing a holy, consecrated life by setting myself apart for God's use so others will see God in me.

December 22 – In God We Trust

In God have I put my trust: I will not be afraid what man can do unto me. Psalm 56:11

'In God have I put my trust, I will not be afraid; what can man do unto me?' — Amp

Fearless now, I trust in God; what can mere mortals do to me? — Message

In God (I will praise His word), In Jehovah (I will praise His word), in God have I put my trust, I will not be afraid; what can man do unto me? — ASV

In God will I praise with good cause: in Yahweh will I praise with good cause; in God have I trusted, I will not fear. What can a son of earth do unto me? — Rhm

In God, whose word I praise, in the Lord, whose word I praise, in God I trust without a fear. What can man do to me? — RSV

I decree I am putting my trust and confidence in God. I decree I am certain He cares for me. I decree I am not afraid of what mere man can do to me because God is protecting me.

December 23 – Jubilant With Joy

But let the righteous be glad; let them rejoice before God; yea, let them exceedingly rejoice. Psalm 68:3

But let the [uncompromisingly] righteous be glad; let them be in high spirits and glory before God, yes, let them [jubilantly] rejoice! — Amp

When the righteous see God in action they'll laugh, they'll sing, they'll laugh and sing for joy. — Message

But the virtuous will be happy; they will be joyful in the Divine presence, and radiant with contentment. — Har

But let them who are righteous rejoice - let them shout for joy at the presence of God - let them be transported with gladness. — Sept

But let the righteous be joyful; let them exult before God; let them be jubilant with joy! — RSV

I decree I am righteous, and I am exceedingly glad. I decree I am full of joy. I decree I am singing and rejoicing in God's goodness, and my mouth is full of laughter. I decree my spirits are high, and I am radiant with contentment.

December 24 – Speak True Words

Hear: for I will speak of excellent things; and the opening of my lips shall be right things.
Proverbs 8:6

Hear, for I will speak excellent and princely things; and opening of my lips shall be for right things. — Amp

You'll only hear true and right words from my mouth; not one syllable will be twisted or skewed. — Message

Hear for I will speak truth; and the opening of my mouth shall bring forth uprightness. — Lam

Harken, for I will speak advisedly; and the announcement of my lips shall be of right things. — Sprl

Hear, for princely things will I speak. And the opening of my lips shall be of equity. — Rhm

I decree when I speak, the right words and words of truth are coming from my mouth. I decree I am speaking words that are only excellent, true, and right. I decree my words are edifying to build up myself and others.

December 25 – A Savior Is Born

For unto you is born this day in the city of David a Saviour, which is Christ the Lord. Luke 2:11

For to you is born this day in the town of David a Savior, Who is Christ (the Messiah) the Lord! — Amp

A Saviour has just been born in David's town, a Savior who is Messiah and Master. — Message

Today in the city of David a deliverer has been born to you - the Messiah, the Lord. — NEB

...the Lord Christ Himself. — Knox

...who is the Anointed Lord. — Mon

...who is your Messiah and Lord. — Wms

I decree I am living my life with my Savior, Jesus, who is the Christ, the Lord. I decree He is the Anointed One. I decree Father God sent His only Son, Jesus, to the earth to be the Savior for me and the world.

December 26 – Live In Vital Union

As ye have therefore received Christ Jesus the Lord, so walk ye in Him. Colossians 2:6

As you have therefore received Christ, [even] Jesus the Lord, [so] walk (regulate your lives and conduct yourselves) in union with and conformity to Him. — Amp

My counsel for you is simple and straight-forward: Just go ahead with what you've been given. You received Christ Jesus, the Master; now live Him. — Message

So just as you once accepted the Christ, Jesus, as your Lord, you must live in vital union with Him. — Gspd

Go on, then ordering your lives in Christ Jesus our Lord, according to the tradition you have received of Him. — Knox

And now just as you trusted Christ to save you, trust Him too for each day's problems; live in vital union with Him. — Tay

I decree I am conforming my life to the example of Jesus' life. I decree I have accepted Jesus as my Savior and I am living my life in vital union with Him. I decree I am trusting Him with each day's challenges.

December 27 – Put On The New

And have put on the new man, which is renewed in knowledge after the image of Him that created him. Colossians 3:10

And have clothed yourselves with the new [spiritual self], which is [ever in the process of being] renewed and remolded into [fuller and more perfect knowledge upon] knowledge after the image (the likeness) of Him Who created it. — Amp

Now you're dressed in a new wardrobe. Every item of your new way of life is custom-made by the Creator, with His label on it. All the old fashions are obsolete. — Message

And have begun life as the new man who is out to learn what he ought to be according to the plan of God. — Phi

...that is being refitted all the time for closer knowledge, so that the image of the God who created it is its pattern. — Knox

I decree I am putting off the old spiritual man and putting on the new spiritual man. I decree old ways of thinking and doing are gone. I am renewing my mind and changing my actions to be more like Jesus.

December 28 – No Distinction

Even the righteousness of God which is by faith of Jesus Christ unto all and upon all them that believe: for there is no difference. Romans 3:22

Namely, the righteousness of God which comes by believing with personal trust and confident reliance on Jesus Christ (the Messiah). [And it is meant] for all who believe. For there is no distinction. — Amp

The God-setting-things-right that we read about has become Jesus-setting-things-right for us. And not only for us, but for everyone who believes in Him. For there is no difference between us and them in this. — Message

...which is bestowed, through faith in Jesus Christ, upon all...who believe in Him... — TCNT

...which comes by believing in Jesus Christ. And it is meant for all who have faith... — Mof

I decree I am the righteousness of God because I am believing in, putting my personal trust in, and confidently relying on Jesus Christ. I decree there is no distinction between Jesus and me in God's eyes.

December 29 – Beginning To End

A land which the Lord thy God careth for: the eyes of the Lord thy God are always upon it, from the beginning of the year even unto the end of the year. Deuteronomy 11:12

A land for which the Lord your God cares; the eyes of the Lord your God are always upon it from the beginning of the year to the end of the year. — Amp

It's a land that God, your God, personally tends - He's the gardener - He alone keeps His eye on it all year long. — Message

...a land which Jehovah thy God watcheth over... — Sprl

...so that the Lord your God Himself must be at pains to tend it... — Knox

...continually are the eyes of Yahweh thy God upon it... — Rhm

...on which the Lord your God always keeps His eye... — Tor

I decree my land and I are being watched over and cared for by God. I decree His eyes are on me from the beginning of the year to the end of the year. I decree He is continuously tending to me and personally caring for me.

December 30 – God's Blessings

The blessing of the Lord, it maketh rich, and He adddeth no sorrow with it. Proverbs 10:22

The blessing of the Lord - it makes [truly] rich, and He adds no sorrow with it [neither does toiling increase it]. — Amp

God's blessing makes life rich; nothing we do can improve on God. — Message

The blessings of the Lord bring riches, and there shall be no sorrow in them. — Lam

The blessing of the Lord is on the head of the righteous; it maketh rich and to it no sorrow of heart shall be joined. — Sept

Tis the Eternal's blessing that brings wealth, and never does it bring trouble as well. — Mof

It is the Lord's blessing that brings wealth, and no effort can substitute for it. — NAB

I decree I am living in the fullness of God's blessing on my life. I decree it is making me rich. I decree there is nothing I can do to improve on His blessing. I decree I do not have to toil and put forth extra effort to make my riches increase. I decree there are no sorrows or troubles that come with God's blessing.

December 31 – Unshakeable Peace

These things I have spoken unto you, that in Me ye might have peace. In the world ye shall have tribulation: but be of good cheer; I have overcome the world. John 16:33

I have told you these things, so that in Me you may have [perfect] peace and confidence. In the world you have tribulation and trials and distress and frustration; but be of good cheer [take courage; be confident, certain, un-daunted]! For I have overcome the world. [I have deprived it of power to harm you and have conquered it for you]. — Amp

I've told you all this so that trusting Me, you will be un-shakable and assured, deeply at peace. In this godless world you will continue to experience difficulties. But take heart! I've conquered the world. — Message

...I have conquered the world. — Wms

I decree I am full of God's perfect peace and confi-dence. I decree I am trusting in the finished work of Jesus on the Cross. I decree I am unshakable. I decree I am full of courage because I am victorious. I decree I am overcoming tribulations, trials, frustrations, and distresses. They cannot harm me because Jesus had already conquered them for me.

PRAYER OF SALVATION

If you would like to receive Jesus as your Lord and Savior, pray this prayer to be born again, and filled with the Holy Spirit with evidence of speaking in tongues. Holy Spirit is a person and He is your true source of power.

Heavenly Father, I come to you in the Name of Jesus. Your Word says, *"If you openly declare that Jesus is Lord and believe in your heart that God raised Him from the dead, you will be saved. For it is by believing in your heart that you are made right with God, and it is by openly declaring your faith that you are saved."* Romans 10:9-10 NLT.

God, I am declaring that Jesus is my Lord, and I believe in my heart that You raised Him from the dead.

It is that simple. You are now a born-again child of God.

The Bible says, *"If imperfect parents know how to lovingly take care of their children and give them what they need, how much more will the perfect heavenly Father give the Holy Spirit's fullness when His children ask Him."* Luke 11:13.

I am asking You to fill me with the Holy Spirit. Holy Spirit, rise up within me as I praise God. I expect to speak with other tongues as You give me utterance according to Acts 2:4 which says, *"They were all filled and equipped with the Holy Spirit and were inspired to speak in tongues - empowered by the Spirit to speak in languages they had never learned!"*

Now, worship and praise God as you are filled with the Holy Spirit and speak in your first language, your heavenly language, or other tongues that you have never learned.

ABOUT LUCIA M. CLABORN

Lucia M. Claborn is an innovator with a remarkable ability to use her story and expertise to help you have incredible breakthroughs in your life. She is a coach, author, and speaker using faith-based strategies to help you achieve restoration. She builds your faith to know your true identity so you can live a victorious life.

Lucia has been writing for more than 40 years, with her recent books being available on Amazon as well as countless publishing platforms around the world.

Her weekly podcasts, Secrets to Victorious Living and Victory on the Veranda, encourage listeners around the world by building their faith to walk in victory.

Lucia and her husband Danny live in North Alabama. They have four married children and four grandchildren.

You can find Lucia online at: LuciaClaborn.com
Facebook: Lucia Claborn
Instagram: @Lucia.Claborn
Clubhouse: Living A Lifestyle of Victory Club
Podcasts: Secrets to Victorious Living and Victory on the Veranda

PRODUCTS AVAILABLE FROM LUCIA M. CLABORN

Books
English Version
ABC's Of Who I Am – Decreeing
Who God Says I Am
ABC's Of Who I Am Journal – Decreeing
Who God Says I Am
Your Victory in the Making – 30 Day Devotional
Your Power & Authority in the Making
– 30 Day Devotional
Faith Builders for Victorious Living, 365 Day Devotional –
Decreeing Your Victory
Overcoming: Winning Strategies to Help You Slay
Your Giants
Collected Confidence vol. 1: An Anthology To Empower Women

Spanish Version
ABC's De Quien Soy –Decretando Quién Dice Dios Que Soy
Yo
ABC's De Quien Soy Diario – Decretando Quién Dice Dios
Que Soy
En Vísperas de Tu Victoria – Un Devocional de 30
Días

Podcast
Secrets to Victorious Living
Victory on the Veranda
Listen On Stitcher, Pinterest, iTunes or
your favorite podcast platform.

Course
Hearing The Voice of God

ABOUT THE BOOK

Faith Builders for Victorious Living—Decree Your Victory, 365 Day Devotional is a tool to equip you to decree your desired future into existence with the power of God's Word.

This book will help you build your faith to walk in victory in many areas of your life. Meditating on and decreeing God's Word over your life will build your faith and renew your mind to think like God.

Lucia M. Claborn selected many of her favorite Bible verses on various topics affecting your everyday, walking around life. She uses multiple Bible translations coupled with faith decrees to build your faith to receive God's promises. As you read this book, you will soon realize as a child of God, you have covenant rights and privileges with Jesus, which enables you to have a manifestation of what you are decreeing.

By taking God's Word, which is a seed, and planting it in your heart, which is the soil, and mixing it with your faith, it will produce a harvest of God's goodness and victory in your life. You can live your life in complete health and healing, abundant prosperity, soundness of mind, peace in your heart, victory, and much more if you will decree these blessings over your life.

www.ingramcontent.com/pod-product-compliance
Lightning Source LLC
Chambersburg PA
CBHW060853120626
46553CB00001B/65